THE WITCH
DOCTOR

MICHAEL TEMCHIN, M.D.

THE
WITCH DOCTOR

MEMOIRS OF A PARTISAN

Introduction by Alexander Donat

HOLOCAUST LIBRARY
NEW YORK

Cover Design by Michael Meyerowitz
Printed in the United States of America

Contents

The Gun
And the Scalpel

In prewar Poland the members of the medical profession were held in high esteem. Whether Jew or Gentile, whether in the sophisticated metropolis or in a remote Jewish *shtetl*, the *pan doktor* enjoyed a position of social prominence.

When the Nazi scourge befell the Polish Jews, some 3,000 Jewish physicians became martyrs — and heroes — of the Holocaust. Of these, perhaps the best known in the world today is the pediatrician Henryk Goldschmidt, the saint of the Warsaw ghetto, who attained immortality under his pen name, Janusz Korczak. But Korczak was by no means alone in his heroism and martyrdom. The book *The Martyrdom of Jewish Physicians in Poland*, which appeared in New York in 1963, lists the names of 2,500 Jewish doctors in Poland who are known to have perished in the Holocaust. They met their death in the concentration camps or on deportation trains, in the losing battle against typhus and starvation in the ghettoes, and in the woods and partisan hideouts where they held the scalpel in one hand and the gun in the other, participating in the armed struggle of the Polish Jews against Nazi tyranny.

Many Jewish physicians in Poland were members and leaders of the *Judenrate*, the "Jewish councils" appointed by the Nazi authorities in the ghettos to carry out their orders. Often, they chose death rather than participate even indirectly in the Nazi effort to bring about the "final solution of the Jewish problem." Among the members of the first *Judenrat* in the ghetto of Vilnius (Vilna) were Drs.

Jacob Wygodzki, Dr. Gershon Gershuni, and two other physicians. Dr. Wygodzki, a leader of Vilnius Jewry for many decades, was 86 years old when he openly protested against Nazi brutality and was killed. Dr. Israel Milejkowski, the devoted, selfless leader of the health service in the Warsaw ghetto, died in Treblinka in January, 1943. Drs. Edwin Bieberstein and Arthur Rosenzweig of Cracow perished in Auschwitz. A Dr. Horowitz in Kolomyja took his own life during the final deportation of Jews from his community. Dr. Jakub Lemberg, the head of the *Judenrat* in Zdunska Wola, near Lodz, was ordered to hand over five Jews as hostages to the German authorities. He "elected" himself, his wife and his two children; he and his wife were gunned down on the spot by the *Ghettoleiter*, Hans Biebow. Dr. Alter Nechemia Fuerstenberg, head physician of the hospital in Kostopol, was commanded by the Germans to deliver to them a list of all the Jewish children under his care. He refused to obey the order and was killed together with his wife and child. Dr. Ludwig Fastman, and subsequently Dr. Nathan Szenderowicz, served as *Judenalteste* (chairmen of the *Judenrat*) in the ghetto of Radom. Both of them perished.

The leader of the inmate uprising in Treblinka on August 2, 1943 was Dr. Julian Chorazycki, a man of 57. A prominent laryngologist who had practiced in Warsaw before the war, Dr. Chorazycki was the "chief doctor" of Treblinka. No one suspected, that this taciturn old man (inmates above the age of 50 were a rarity in such places), in his white medical coat with a Red Cross armband, was the mastermind of a desperate rebellion. He was caught quite by accident. The deputy commander of the camp, SS *Oberscharfuehrer* Kurt Franz, who was nicknamed "Lalka" (The Doll) because of his good looks and "Angel

10

of Death" because of his brutality, walked unannounced into Dr. Chorazycki's office and noticed a bulge under the doctor's coat. It was a cache of 750,000 zlotys that somehow had been scraped together by the inmates and turned over to the doctor for the purchase of weapons. With superhuman calm, Dr. Chorazycki reached for a vial and swallowed the poison in it; he feared that he might betray his comrades under torture. He died instantly, and the Germans could learn nothing more about the conspiracy until after it had erupted into a full-scale revolt.

Physicians were prominent also in the resistance groups that grew up in the ghettos. Dr. David Wdowinski, leader of the Zionist Revisionist party in prewar Poland, was the political chief of the Betar Revisionist youth movement and the *Zydowski Zwiazek Wojskowy* (Jewish Military Union) in the Warsaw ghetto. On the other end of the political spectrum was Dr. Henryk Sternhel (known by the underground name of "Gustav"), one of the leaders and chief organizers of the left-wing People's Guard (precursor of the *Armia Ludowa*, the Communist-led "People's Army"). An officer in the Jaroslaw Dabrowski Brigade of the International Brigades that fought in the Spanish Civil war, Dr. Sternhel had fled from Spain to France, where he had been interned. He escaped from the internment camp and arrived in Poland in 1942. As commander of the People's Guard in Warsaw, he set out on April 24, 1943 with three men to help his fellow Jews in the Warsaw ghetto revolt. Two of the three men who planned to scale the ghetto wall with Dr. Sternhel were Jews: Solomon Szlakman (his underground name was Stefan Koluszko) and eighteen-year-old Rysiek Moselman. On Freta Street, near the ghetto wall, they attacked a German police car with hand grenades, killing five gendarmes and remain-

11

ing unharmed themselves. Another Warsaw doctor, Dr. Wlodzimierz Szyfrys, led the Jewish defense organization in the Trawniki camp, where he perished.

One of the best-known Jewish physicians in the ranks of the partisan fighters was Dr. Jechiel Atlas. Born in Rawa Mazowiecka, near Lodz, in 1913, Dr. Atlas had fled with his family into the Soviet-occupied sector of Poland but in 1941 was overtaken by the German forces in the little town of Kozlovshchina, Novogrudok region. In May, 1942 his parents and his sixteen-year-old sister were killed in a massacre by an *Einsatzgruppe* (mobile killing squad). Dr. Atlas made contact with a partisan unit and, together with Boris Bulak, a Soviet partisan, organized a fighting unit of 50 men and a "family camp," where people who had escaped from the ghettos but were too young, too old or too ill to fight hid out from the Germans in the woods, under the protection of the partisan fighters. Eventually, Dr. Atlas' unit merged with other units to form the famous *Pobeda* (Victory) detachment. This fighting group attacked the garrison of Derechin, killing seventeen Germans and six Lithuanian policemen, and subsequently executing forty-four Lithuanians known as murderers of Jews. The *Pobeda* detachment also blew up the railroad bridge over the Nieman river and attacked Kozlovshchina, killing thirty Germans. In a raid on the fortified village of Huta Jaworska, Atlas' comrades killed 127 Germans and collaborators. Late in November, 1942, the Germans launched a massive clean-up operation against the partisans in the Lipchanskaya woods. Dr. Atlas was killed in December, 1942 and was posthumously awarded the title of Hero of the Soviet Union.

Among other Jewish doctors who died fighting in partisan units were Drs. Ahron Filipowski and Berach of Baranowicze; Dr. Melman of Glina; Dr. Markus of

Zdzieciol; Dr. Garber of the Lipczany partisan base; Drs. Abraham Mielnik and Shalom Gerling, who directed a partisan field hospital in the woods; Dr. Rakower of the Nowogrudok ghetto, who served as a medical officer in a partisan unit; Dr. Chaim Munz of Kobryn, and Drs. Alpert, Golombiowski, Pupko and Rosenzweig of *Pobeda* headquarters.

Dr. Michael Temchin, the author of this book, was one of the very few partisan doctors to survive the war. His determination not to be captured alive carried him through many narrow escapes. Drafted into the Polish army as a young doctor in 1939, he became a prisoner of war. Eventually released, he settled in the little town of Grabowiec, in the Lublin region, where he opened a practice. In 1942, when the Jews of Grabowiec were "resettled," he jumped from a train bound for the Sobibor death camp and joined a partisan unit. Before long, thanks to his consummate skill and several fortunate coincidences, he became known among the partisans and the Polish peasants in the neighboring villages not only as a gallant resistance fighter but also as something of a miracle worker — hence his underground name, *Znachor*, literally, "Witch Doctor." Dr. Temchin became a close friend of General Rola Zymierski, commander in chief of the *Armia Ludowa,* and eventually was named chief medical officer of the *AL*'s Lublin regional command.

This book is Michael Temchin's personal memoir of his years as a partisan fighter. In low-key, understated language, he recalls his experiences from 1939 to 1947. He tells of saving a baby that had been snatched from its mother as she boarded the deportation train. One of the reasons why he risked his life to rescue the infant, he explains, was in order to prove to himself that in the midst of inhumanity and terror, he could still remain a human be-

13

ing capable of affirming life. Apparently blessed with an iron constitution, Dr. Temchin, hit by German shrapnel, himself prepared and applied a plaster cast to his broken wrist. In the partisan camp, he organized a "medical corps" and a "nurses' school," One of his nurses was a girl of thirteen.

Dr. Temchin has much to tell about the beginnings of the Polish partisan movement, the role played in it by Jews, and the conflicts between the resistance organizations formed by various political parties that hoped to assume power in Poland after the war.

Following the liberation of Poland, Dr. Temchin seemed to be set for a brilliant career in the army of the Polish People's Republic. He was called in to join a team of doctors — he was a major, all the others were generals — that visited Prime Minister Wladyslaw Gomulka when the latter came down with a baffling ailment. Then, in 1947, his father-in-law, Dr. Emil Sommerstein, the leader of Poland's postwar Jewish community, visited the United States heading a delegation of the Polish Jews to seek help for the surviving remnants. On the day he was to return to Poland, Dr. Sommerstein was felled by a paralytic stroke. Dr. Temchin and his wife and their young son set sail for the United States to be at the sick man's side. Dr. Sommerstein never recovered from his illness, and the Temchins settled in the United States. Dr. Temchin practiced in Brooklyn for several years, then moved to the small town of Florida in upstate New York, where he was active as a physican until his retirement in 1977.

The Witch Doctor is a brief but for this very reason all the more poignant saga of the heroism of a Jewish physician in the Polish resistance movement during the Holocaust period.

14   **Alexander Donat**

For my wife Mira,
and children Shelley and Jack

Foreword

The Union of Jewish Partisans was formed in Poland in 1945. On that occasion General Rola-Zymierski, the Chief of Staff of the Polish Army sent a letter of congratulations to the President of the organization.

In this letter he acknowledged that in spite of the worst conditions which the Jewish People had endured during the German occupation, they had never lost their fighting spirit.

The Jews produced, he went on, fighters of the first caliber, fighters such as Col. Gustaw Alef ("Bolek"), Lieutenant-Colonel Michael Temchin ("Znachor"), Major Witek Margulies ("Felek"), Chil Grynszpan, Mietek Gruber, etc. He paid homage to the Jewish heroes who gave their lives in the fight of unequal forces: Major Skotnicki ("Zemsta"), Niuta Teitelbaum ("Wanda"), and others.

There were others, many of them. There were Jews in the Home Army (Armia Krajowa), as well as in the Polish People's Army (PAL), but they had to hide their Jewishness for fear of being rejected or persecuted. Many of them perished and their names and deeds are forever lost to the Jewish People. Many of these fighters survived and have chosen never to reveal their Jewishness. They continue to live under their assumed names.

Six million Jews disappeared in Europe—what were their stories? What did they have to tell us before Nazi death took them away? Nobody will ever be able to imagine.

It is the survivors' duty to bear witness to Jewish suffering, humiliation, sacrifice and herosim. And it is in this spirit that this memoir is being offered.

ACKNOWLEDGMENTS

My gratitude goes to Mr. Alexander Donat for encouraging me to write these memoirs and the thoughtful attention he gave to the manuscript.

I also appreciate the help of Miss Susan Kusiek for her typing of the manuscript.

The Author

CHAPTER ONE

The
Beginning

I was born on August 5, 1909 in Pinsk, Poland, where I grew up. My parents, Szejna and Jacob, were, among others, the backbone of the Jewish Socialist party, the "Bund." From them I inherited a strong attachment to the Yiddish language and everything Jewish, although none of us were basically religious people.

After graduation, first from a *Yiddish Folkshule* (Yiddish-language secular school) and later from a state high school, and after serving for fifteen months in the Polish army, I was accepted at the medical school in Warsaw. I was graduated as a doctor of medicine in 1937. Three years earlier, in 1934, I had married my high school sweetheart, Mania Feldman. We had no children. On March 23, 1939, within hours after Hitler's infamous "Danzig" speech, I was mobilized into the Polish army once again and sent to the German border in Pomerania.

The outbreak of the war found me in Brest Litovsk, an old Polish fortress. From there I was sent to the front in the Bialystok region as chief of a unit in charge of evacuating the wounded and sick of the 9th Infantry Division. After three weeks of combat I was taken prisoner. At first a few doctors and I were attached to a German front-line medical unit. We followed the battle lines and were assigned to care for the Polish casualties. At the end of September, 1939, I was appointed one of the three physicians in a transit camp for prisoners of war in Rastenburg, a small town in East Prussia, later the site of one of Hitler's most

19

elaborate fortress-bunkers. When this temporary camp was liquidated, I was given the task of organizing an infirmary in a small town, Gerdauen, for Polish POWs and civilians working in German factories and farms. We were treated comparatively well. The local population, many of them of Polish extraction, were quite friendly. Gerdauen was only about ten miles from the Lithuanian border and we were not guarded too strictly. Four noncommissioned officers and I decided to make a run for the border in one of the eighteen cars parked in our yard. But one of the men in our group gave us away and I, the only commissioned officer in the group, was arrested and "interrogated" by the local police and the Gestapo for about two weeks. Primarily they were eager to know where I had gotten the compass and the map they had found on me. I had received it from one of the guards. Despite the harsh interrogation, I did not break down. I insisted that I did not know who the man had been. I said I had seen him only once and that he was not on guard duty now.

Had this incident happened six or twelve months later, I would not have lived to tell it, but at this early stage of the war, two factors in my favor saved my life. First, the Germans were still comparatively lenient toward prisoners of war and adhered to some of the international laws regarding the treatment of POWs. Secondly, a few weeks earlier, a representative of the International Red Cross had visited my infirmary. He had written down my name and the address of my wife and my father. He even took a letter from me to them in Pinsk. So I was on the Red Cross list of POWs and the Germans could not simply do away with me. But I received my punishment. On January 1, 1940, I was sent to the "mother camp," Stalag IA. This camp had its main offices and hospital in the town of Stablak. The camp itself was in a place called Guerken.

The inmates of Stalag IA were housed in wooden barracks and grouped according to nationalities. There was a compound for *Volksdeutsche* (ethnic Germans), a Polish compound, a Ukrainian compound, a White Russian compound, and, of course, a separate compound for Jews. All the prisoners were treated like animals, but the inmates of the Jewish compound were the most abused.

There was one more compound, the "penal compound." This was an international compound that housed all kinds of criminals — thieves, rapists, murderers — along with suspected spies, saboteurs, political prisoners and fugitives. The conditions in the "penal compound" defied the imagination. Hard labor, starvation and fatal beatings were the order of the day. Suffice it to say that when I first arrived at the "penal compound," we were about 800 inmates; when I left, three months later, only about 300 of these were still alive.

During the three months I spent at Stalag IA I became very weak. I suffered from diarrhea and was literally eaten alive by scabies and lice. I lost a great deal of weight. I had never been a large man, but at Stalag IA, I came down to about forty-five or fifty kilograms. Nevertheless, I fought and held on.

In the middle of March, 1940, Jews who had lived in the part of Poland that had been occupied by the Russians were repatriated. Although my native city, Pinsk, was now in the Soviet sector, I was initially excluded from the transport and left in the "penal compound" as a fugitive.

On March 31, 1940, I was summoned to the infirmary. I was told that a German doctor, Major Clemens Hantel, was looking for a physician who could speak several languages, namely German, Polish, Russian, French and Ukrainian. Luck was on my side; none of the doctors in the infirmary or the hospital spoke all these languages. Among the Jewish POWs there was one Dr. Henryk Dlugi, who decided that this might be an opportunity to get me out of the "penal compound." He told the Germans that there was one physician who knew several languages. As a result, an orderly was sent to my barrack to bring me and all my belongings to the infirmary at once.

The Germans looked me over, asked a few questions regarding my linguistic skills and told me to put my things into the car. I asked Dr. Dlugi where I was going. He did not know but thought that in any other place I would have a better chance of survival than in the penal compound.

We left and three hours later I became the attending physician in a beautiful Catholic hospital in charge of about 6,000 French and Polish POWs and civilians doing forced labor in factories, on road construction projects and on farms.

The seven months I spent in St. Joseph's Hospital in Guttstadt are among the most memorable experiences of my life. I had an entire ward in the hospital for the use of my patients. All diagnostic and therapeutic facilities were at my disposal. Also, in another building, I had a wing for contagious diseases. My food and living quarters were first class, comparable to private accommodations. In addition, as a second lieutenant, I was paid a salary of seventy-two marks a month. Dr. Hantel was always available for consultations.

Late in September, 1940, the Germans gathered all the Jewish POWs of this region into one large camp in a place called Hammerstein. From there, we were told, we would

22

be sent to the German-occupied sector of Poland, where we would be officially discharged from the army and be able to start a normal civilian life. We all waited eagerly for this promise to come true.

* * *

One day we were given each one loaf of bread and some marmalade meant to last us three or four days. Our journey was uneventful, and we were full of anticipation. We were singing and joking, eager to see our loved ones again.

At last, we arrived at our destination, Biala Podlaska. Immediately we were surrounded by SS and *Sonderkommandos*, special details made up of Latvians, Estonians and Ukrainians. We became civilians, but we were herded into one of the worst labor camps imaginable run by the SS. There were two more doctors with me: Dr. Bronislaw Wislicki and Dr. Majem, a pediatrician from Lwow.

Conditions at this camp were even worse than at the "penal compound" in Stalag IA. Not a day passed without some Jews being beaten, starved, or worked to death for the slightest infraction of rules (what rules?). The greatest amusement for the guards was practice shooting at moving targets: the Jews working in the fields. We were given virtually no food, but we ourselves became food for lice, scabies and rats. People died like flies.

I did not stay long at Biala Podlaska. After about three weeks I went, as usual, to the field where we collected rocks, dug ditches and filled them in again, but instead of returning to the camp at the end of the day, I boarded the first train to Warsaw and arrived there two days before the ghetto was ordered closed.

In Warsaw, I found many acquaintances and friends.

Dr. Stephanie Mesh (Palew) and Dr. George Kiriasefer were the ones that helped me the most. I lived with a family Gothelf on Ciepla Street.

At the end of December, 1940, I volunteered to leave the ghetto of Warsaw and go to a small town, Warka, near Radom, to fight an epidemic of typhoid fever and typhus among the Jewish population. In Warka, I was invited to stay with Osher Wertshauser and his family. These wonderful people treated me like a long-lost relative. Under my direction, the Jews in Warka built a public bath with a delousing room. I also organized a small hospital for infectious diseases that made life bearable, but this did not last long.

One day, at the end of February, 1941, the order came: The entire Jewish community was to assemble at the market place at six o'clock the next morning. They would be permitted to take with them only things they could carry in their hands; nothing else. Those who failed to report would be summarily shot. The doctor, meaning me, was to remain at the hospital until all the patients would be able to travel. By 6:30 the town had been cleared. I was told that the Germans were consolidating all the small ghettos into one large ghetto that would become autonomous.

Three days later, I received new orders. I was to bring all my patients from the hospital to Grojec, a town near Warka. From there, we were evacuated, along with the Jews of Grojec, back to Warsaw.

The situation in Warsaw was unbearable. People were dying in the streets; those who survived were in constant danger of being seized for slave labor. The city was overcrowded. At first I could not find a job and I literally led the life of a beggar. Again, my main towers of strength were the Kiriasefers and the Meshes.

In June, 1941, I left Warsaw. At the suggestion of Dr. Jacob Feldman, a *landsman* of mine from Pinsk and a good friend, I decided to start a practice in Grabowiec, a small town between Hrubieszow and Zamosc. I arrived there on June 20, 1941. Two days later, the Germans attacked Russia.

When Pinsk was occupied by the Germans, I tried to get there to be with Mania and my father, but this was impossible. I had to remain in Grabowiec, which had a Jewish quarter in the slums. Since this was not a sealed ghetto, there were no restrictions on movements between the Jewish and Aryan sectors of the town during the daytime.

The Gentile population of Grabowiec consisted of Poles and Ukrainians.

When I first arrived in Grabowiec, there were two other physicians left in the town. The one was a Ukrainian, Dr. Stankow, an older man, who was very friendly; the other was a Pole, also an old man, who, unlike Stankow, was hostile from the moment I introduced myself to him.

Officially, I was permitted to treat only Jews, but in fact most of my patients were Christians, including local officials — Polish police, *Kripo (Kriminalpolizei* or plainclothesmen), and employees of the bailiff's office, whom I never charged a fee for treating them and their families. My generosity put me in their good graces. Generally, I was not strict about fees. I never overcharged anyone; in many instances, I gave my services free of charge. As a result, a lot of good will developed between the townspeople and myself. I made many good friends. Among my best friends were two sisters who owned the local pharmacy. (The pharmacist, Mr. Antonowicz, had been taken to Auschwitz as a political prisoner the day after my arrival in Grabowiec. He was to perish there.) I was also on excel-

25

lent terms with Koprowski, the town butcher, and his family, and many others, whose names I can no longer remember. I cannot recall anyone who would have wanted to denounce me to the Germans.

My host in town until I could find a place of my own was a Jew known as Leyzer the Tailor. (I never learned his last name and I don't think anyone else knew.) It was Leyzer who accompanied me on my first house call, which came when I had hardly got off the wagon that had brought me to Grabowiec.

The patient was a middle-aged woman who was suffering from severe shortness of breath, swelling of the legs, and all the other symptoms of heart failure. After examining her, I asked to see the medication she had been taking. (It had been prescribed by the pharmacist who had been taken to Auschwitz.) It turned out to be exactly what I myself would have prescribed. I told the woman to continue taking the medication and be patient. I then collected my fee of ten zlotys and left.

But Leyzer the Tailor was upset. "Doctor," he said, "this woman has already been taking this medication for two or three weeks without getting any better. I don't want to teach you your business but in my opinion, you should at least have added some sugar or salt to the prescription to make it taste different. Now they will say you are just as bad a doctor as the last one. Maybe you don't even know how to write a prescription!"

Leyzer probably was right. In a *shtetl*, news traveled fast and once you got a bad reputation, nothing could change it. I became discouraged but hope returned when I was invited to a full-time course Jewish dinner by Leyzer's wife. After the last course, a jigger of liquor, 96 per cent proof, Leyzer the Tailor started to console me.

26

"You'll make a living here and you can stay with us as long as necessary."

I spent the next day making plans for my future in case things did not work out for me in Grabowiec. At about five o'clock that afternoon a girl came and asked me to see her uncle, who lived several houses away from Leyzer's. She said she wanted me to come as soon as possible because the *feldsher* was waiting; he wanted to have a "consultation" with me. What kind of *feldsher*? I wondered. I knew that there was no other Jewish doctor in town.

The profession of *feldsher* was very popular in eastern Poland and in Russia, where there was a chronic shortage of qualified doctors. The basic education of a *feldsher* was similar to the training of a nurse. *Feldshers* worked at hospitals and acquired practical experience in diagnosing certain ailments, particularly infectious diseases. They were quite adept at examining patients and could make good use of percussion and auscultation. But to consult with a *feldsher* was considered beneath the professional dignity of a physician.

However, despite my own reservations, I told myself, "To hell with professional pride." The ten zlotys in my pocket would come in handy. Several minutes later I entered the patient's home.

The first thing to hit me was a terrible stench. There was a crowd of people in the room. All the windows were closed; the heat was unbearable. Also, the air was filled with the smoke of cheap tobacco.

When I got sufficiently hardened to the atmosphere to look around me, I saw a man lying in the bed. At the foot of the bed sat an elderly man, who was neatly dressed and who introduced himself to me as Yisroel Rayner, the *feldsher*.

I announced that I would not examine the patient until all the windows had been opened and everybody else had left the room. There appeared to be some opposition, but when it was clear that the *feldsher* approved of my request, the people obeyed.

Here I should add a few words about this *feldsher*, who was known in town as Reb Yisroel. He had been born in Grabowiec but, after becoming a *feldsher*, twenty-five years earlier, he had set up practice in another small town, Dubienka, which had now been occupied by the Russians. Reb Yisroel had arrived in Grabowiec on the same day as I and had moved back into his old house.

After exchanging niceties with Reb Yisroel, I turned to the patient. He was an emaciated, ascetic-looking young man with bushy, black hair and a long beard that made him look even paler than he was. He did not look at me but I heard him murmuring prayers in Yiddish that all the angels should be at my side because it was God Himself who had sent me.

He said he had always been a healthy man, strong and hardworking. At another time or in another place, he would have belonged to a "Polar Bear Club." He liked to go out in the winter, chop a hole into the ice that covered the nearby lake and bathe in the frigid water. His illness had begun in February, following one of those ice baths. He had been seen by all the doctors in the neighborhood, Jewish and Gentile. He even had been sent to a hospital in Lublin, but no one could find the cause of his trouble. In the meantime, his condition had continued to deteriorate. It was suggested that he might have tuberculosis, hepatitis, or some rare disease of the blood. He had been treated for all these, but to no avail.

I examined the man very thoroughly. I found nothing to account for his condition except that there seemed to be differences between the bases of the lungs. I suspected that he had some fluid at the base of one lung. Reb Yisroel agreed — or pretended to agree — with my findings.

I spent more than an hour with the patient. Then I called in his parents and explained the situation. In order to make sure that my suspicions were correct, I would have to insert a needle into the suspected area to see what was there. However, I suggested that we wait to do that until the next day because the patient was very tired.

The parents paid me my ten zlotys and told me they would let me know whether I would still be needed the next day. Apparently, that decision would be made by Reb Yisroel, and I felt that he would be on my side.

This time Leyzer the Tailor was satisfied. "It was smart to make two visits out of one," he said.

"Reb Yisroel will be difficult to beat," Leyzer the Tailor told me. "He is a local man and everybody thinks he's smart, too. The peasants call him the 'Jewish doctor of Grabowiec.' But we shall see what happens tomorrow."

The next day was one of long drawn-out suspenseful waiting. I made up my mind that if I would not be called to see this patient again I would give up on Grabowiec and move to Hrubieszow or Zamosc.

At about four o'clock that afternoon, my patient's niece turned up with the announcement that Reb Yisroel was now with her uncle and waiting to have a "consultation" with me. I picked up my medical bag (which contained a stethoscope, one 2cc syringe, plus both my needles — one for intramuscular injections, the other, a very long one, the kind ordinarily used only in veterinary medicine) and was on my way.

Once again the room was full of people and the windows were closed. The patient's mother explained that she had closed them to keep her son from catching a cold in addition to whatever else was wrong with him. Once again I had to send away all the spectators and open the windows. When the smoke cleared, I began to work on my patient. I boiled the syringe and both needles in a frying pan.

I again examined the patient. I was sure there was fluid somewhere. I inserted the large needle into the patient's body, aiming at the lower part of the right pleural sac, and I prayed for some kind of fluid to come out. Meanwhile, my patient, too, was murmuring some sort of prayer, over and over again.

Suddenly the door flew open and a crowd poured into the room with shouts of "Oh, what a doctor! What a genius! A real professor! He guessed it right the very first time!" I didn't know what had happened. Then I looked at the syringe. It was full of gray, smelly pus. I removed the syringe, leaving the needle in place. The pus continued to pour out. In this way, I evacuated a large amount of pus and other debris. The patient immediately felt better and I was able to make a diagnosis. He was suffering from an abscess near the kidney.

I explained that the patient would need an operation. "Fine," said the family. "Go right ahead. Our house is clean. We also have clean towels and good knives. We'll all help." It took some talking by me and Reb Yisroel to convince the family that the patient would have to go to the nearest hospital, which was in Hrubieszow. There, with the assistance of my friend Dr. Feldman, I performed the operation and put in a drain to draw out the remaining infected matter. The patient recovered — only to perish a few months later in the gas chamber at Sobibor.

My correct "guess" of this illness established my credentials as a good doctor. That same afternoon I made eighteen house calls and a lot of money. At least some of the credit for my success goes to Reb Yisroel, who accompanied me on all the house calls and became a kind of assistant to me. My practice grew steadily, especially among the Gentile population. I saw to it that Reb Yisroel's own practice remained intact; I praised him and frequently called him to help me. Moreover, I gave him advice in cases he was not competent to handle and I approved his prescriptions. Reb Yisroel and Leyzer the Tailor became two of my best friends in Grabowiec. Reb Yisroel felt I had helped him retain his old title, "the Jewish doctor of Grabowiec." "You could have ruined us," he and his wife kept saying. "Yet you helped us keep up our practice. How will we ever repay you for what you did for us?"

(Alas, if what I learned after the war was true, Reb Yisroel repaid me literally with his own life. It seems that, following the liquidation of the Grabowiec ghetto, he and his family were caught by the Germans near the town of Izbica. By that time the Germans were hot on my trail, too, because I had acquired some notoriety as a partisan leader in and around Grabowiec. And so, when Reb Yisroel was identified as "the Jewish doctor of Grabowiec," the Germans believing that they had captured me at long last, murdered him and his family, and ceased to look for me.)

I was very well liked not only in Grabowiec but also by the people in the surrounding villages. I began to hope that I would survive the war in Grabowiec. But life was to create a different scenario for me.

CHAPTER TWO

Baby S.

Grabowiec was a small town with a population of about 5,000. As I have already said, most of the people were Poles and Ukrainians. There were also about 1,700 Jews. The Gentiles were mostly farmers, butchers and saloon-keepers. The Jewish population was typical of the *shtetl*; most of there were tradesmen, carpenters, shoemakers and tailors. There were many peddlers and a few individuals with "legitimate" businesses.

During the first months of the German occupation the relationships among the various nationality groups were, to say the least, correct except for a few episodes of name-calling and threats. But in the beginning of 1940, all the Jews had been forced to abandon their homes and move into the ghetto, However, as I have already mentioned, people were permitted to move in and out freely during the day. Restrictions imposed by the Germans were not enforced too strictly by the local police or the *Kripo*, the German plainclothesmen. Some of the officials periodically threatened to enforce the German laws in order to obtain certain favors from the Jews. However, the *Judenrat* usually paid off these individuals and life went on.

In 1941, the year I arrived there, the Jewish population of Grabowiec increased considerably, due to an influx of refugees from larger communities. Living conditions became increasingly difficult because of overcrowding and dire poverty. The *Judenrat* set up a public soup kitchen, where one could get one meal a day. Some refugees found shelter with local families. Life was still bearable.

In the spring of 1942, a contingent of gendarmes was sent into Grabowiec to fight bands of armed Russian prisoners of war who had escaped and were operating in the woods nearby. These groups were not really organized partisans. They had sought refuge in the woods and, in order to survive, stole food and clothing, mostly from peasants in isolated farmsteads. Occasionally they would raid farms managed by the Germans.

It became the duty of the Jewish population to furnish the gendarmes with lodging, food and furniture. The *Judenrat* was also obliged to supply the Germans with housekeepers, cooks and servants, who had to be young and attractive women. They were treated like slaves. Rape by two or three men was the order of the day. One girl of twelve was so badly mauled during such an "act of collective love" that she required about five or six stitches to restore her into halfway human shape. Another girl had the audacity to become pregnant and carry a "German" in her Jewish womb. This was a crime punishable by death. Luckily, she did not live long enough for the Germans to find out about it.

Speaking of children, Jewish people in the ghettos did not have any babies. The youngest children were those born during the first months of the war. After that, Jewish women did not bear children. They avoided pregnancies; if they conceived, abortions were quite easy to arrange. All the doctors helped, especially the Jewish doctors.

But in the Grabowiec ghetto there was one baby. Mrs. S., originally from Lodz, refused to kill her unborn offspring, and, at the time of the story I am about to tell, the infant, a girl, was approximately three months old. The Jewish community, after its initial displeasure with what normally would have been welcomed as a "blessed event," took the baby to its heart. Everyone felt like a parent to this child, cherishing it as a reminder that Jews were still alive, not only empty shells, vegetables without a future, without self-respect. The baby received the best of care, many presents, and almost daily medical checkups from the doctor, namely, myself.

By this time I had become a respected member of the community, popular among both Jews and Gentiles, including the chief of the gendarmerie, whom I was secretly treating for gonorrhea.

Conditions in the ghetto gradually deteriorated after one of the gendarmes was killed during a hunt for "bandits." The Germans were afraid to enter the woods, but they had to pacify the area. They had to show some results of their work, and so they found an easy way out, Every so often they would select at random several Jews, mostly newcomers to the town, and shoot them publicly, announcing that these had been "bandits." Later, they did not even bother to look for newcomers. They simply assembled Jews at random and executed them in order to "set an example." This practice was safe, easy, and, in the eyes of the higher authorities, good work. After a while, the Jews learned to live with this situation also, sustained by the hope each time that they wouldn't be next and that there soon would be good news about German defeats on the battlefront. They took comfort also from the fact that in other towns the ghettos had been sealed so that life was much more difficult to endure there than in Grabowiec.

The Jews in Grabowiec clung to every vestige of hope, to every sign that could be construed as hope. They closed their eyes and ears to everything that was bad. When news came of "resettlements" and "deportations" from other communities, and rumors spread about annihilation camps, the Jews dismissed them as propaganda, even though, in their hearts, they suspected that the rumors were based on fact. "They simply can't kill millions of people," the Jews argued. "Not in this century, not in such a civilized nation." Besides, the world would not allow such a crime to occur. There still was, after all, an America, an England. There was world opinion. No! No! Such horror stories were only figments of the minds of degenerates and criminals who wanted to exploit the misery of the Jews.

And so, life went on.

* * *

Then, on June 8, 1942, it happened. The chairman of the *Judenrat* was summoned to the gendarmerie and told that all the Jews of Grabowiec would have to be assembled on the lawn in front of *Judenrat* headquarters by six o'clock that evening. They could take with them anything they could carry in their hands. No further explanations were given. The order, it was emphasized, would be stringently enforced. Any Jew caught in a place other than on the lawn after six o'clock would be shot on sight. No hint was given of things to come. No one asked. Everyone knew. "Resettlement," deportations, labor camps, annihilation camps? There was a wide variety of choices . . . which was better? Which would it be?

There was no panic. Silently, the Jews packed whatever they felt they would need the most. Mothers and fathers, holding back tears, gave their children answers they themselves did not believe. People put on their best clothes. Despite the heat, some put on their overcoats and even winter clothes, in order to be able to take as many of their possessions as possible into the unknown future.

At six o'clock, everyone was in place. Very few people disobeyed the order. The lawn in front of *Judenrat* headquarters was crowded with people, packages and suitcases. *Judenrat* officials walked about checking lists. People were yelling, children were crying. The lawn, green and inviting only a few hours earlier, now looked like one huge refugee camp, just like those that could be seen in towns and villages where the first bombs had fallen and the inhabitants had escaped with little more than their lives.

Before dark, the lawn was surrounded by gendarmes. A high-ranking SS officer appeared. He was short, immaculately dressed, pompous and very sure of himself, looking with contempt at the crowd of "subhumans" before him. The secretary of the *Judenrat*, Mr. Abramson, received his final instructions. The Germans, he was told, had decided to consolidate all the smaller ghettos in the area into one large Jewish settlement in the town of Hrubieszow, not far away. There, the Jews would be on their own, a self-governing entity, a kind of "Jewish state," protected against persecution from the Gentile populace. There they would be given employment and earn their livelihood by honest, sweaty work, not by speculation or by exploitation of others, as they had done before. There was nothing to fear, the SS officer assured the *Judenrat* official. "And now you all had better get some rest," he concluded, "because early tomorrow morning all you people will march to the railroad station, about ten kilometers from here, and board the special trains that will take you to your new homes."

That summer night was beautiful. The air was fresh, the skies were clear. To an outsider the scene might have appeared like a peaceful evening after a big community picnic. People stood in small groups; friends and families huddled together, talking in whispers. There was an occasional sigh; a few people seemed to be praying, but the mood seemed calm. As the night wore on, an uneasy silence descended on the lawn, broken only from time to time by laughter from a nearby building where the gendarmes were spending the night. Once in a while there was a distant burst of machine-gun fire. Probably a Jew had been caught in the town and instant German justice had been administered.

None of us paid much attention to such "little" things. People were immersed in their own thoughts. Some had fallen asleep. The only sign of life that could be seen from afar was the flickering of a match lighting a cigarette in the darkness. Finally the blackness of the night took over. Everything seemed peaceful and serene.

* * *

In the first crimson rays of the rising sun, the lawn still gave the impression of the morning after an outdoor celebration, with the guests resting from the festivities of the night before. Soon, however, the true picture of what was about to happen became clear. Several horse-drawn wagons, driven by peasants from the surrounding countryside, came into view. A cordon of gendarmes surrounded the lawn.

All at once the quiet turned into an inferno of agitation. The sick and the old were loaded onto the peasant wagons. The procedure was speeded up with blows from fists and rifle butts and kicks from heavy boots. Those able to walk were ordered to form a column. All this was accompanied by the whistle of whips and the raucous shouts of the Germans, *"Schneller! Schneller! Heraus! Heraus, verfluchte Juden!"* ("Faster! Step on it! Out! Out, you damned Jews!") The idyllic picture of the evening before had turned into a scenario of sheer hell.

The sun shone brightly. It promised to be a beautiful day. But this did not give any comfort to us, the condemned.

At last, the march began. I kept well in the rear of the marching column. When I passed the last building of Grabowiec, I took one final look back. Grabowiec had never been a pretty place; now it looked altogether like a ghost town. The unpaved roads were dirty, and the empty shacks were falling apart. From outside, I could see broken beds, tables good only for firewood, and window frames torn from their hinges. A deep silence enveloped Grabowiec, broken only by the creaking of doors and windows slammed by the wind.

Each of us was, or pretended to be, occupied with private thoughts of his or her own. Some of the marchers really believed that a brighter future was waiting for them. I knew better, I had already survived four "resettlements" and had not yet become accustomed to them, for in each "resettlement" I lost people who were close and dear to me.

All we knew for certain was our immediate destination, the railroad station. Whether we were really going to Hrubieszow, and if so, what would await us there — who could tell? But there was no time for thinking. Whoever slowed down, fell back or collapsed vanished from the column. What happened to them? No one really wanted to find out. No one even wanted to speculate. But there was

41

always a muffled cracking noise from a distance, and usually later a gendarme would appear, cleaning his gun and replacing it in its holster.

After about three hours, we reached our destination, the Mionchin railroad station. To our right was the station building, then a wide empty space, fenced off from the town with barbed wire. Farther to the left, a considerable distance from the railroad tracks, stood warehouses, gray, dirty and dilapidated.

The wagons bearing the elderly, the sick and the young children were directed toward the empty space in front of the warehouses. There, they were unloaded. Whoever could not jump off the wagons was thrown off. No one was given any help, nor did anyone ask for it. A cry for help would only have shown that one was worthless, and it would have led to a beating or perhaps even worse. At last the wagons were empty. The horses were led into the shade of the warehouses. There they were given oats and water. No such sustenance was given to the human cargo they had pulled.

Our column was ordered to a halt in the wide area between the main building of the station and the warehouses. A "reception committee" was already waiting for us there. In addition to the SS officer we had seen on the lawn the night before, and who seemed to be directing the entire operation, there was the *Kreishauptmann* (county official) with his aides and a very attractive young blonde German woman. There were also German administrators who ran large farms and estates that had been confiscated from their Polish owners. And wherever one looked, there were gendarmes.

A preliminary "selection" began on the spot. The obviously sick, the old, and very young children were pushed out of the group and assembled near the railroad tracks, in the hot sun, and ordered to keep quiet. Those who did not move fast enough, or did not seem to have understood the instructions, were beaten into obedience with whips, rifles and kicks of German boots. A contingent of gendarmes was left to guard them. At the least sign of commotion, a gendarme rushed to the spot to restore *Ordnung*, and the ones found guilty were brought into line by well-aimed punches of a fist or a rifle butt.

Meanwhile, the young and healthy Jews were subjected to an appraisal. The men were separated from the women, and then the appropriation of slave laborers began. The *Kreishauptmann* carried a cane with a semi-circular handle, with which he would catch a young man or woman by the neck, pull his victim out of the crowd and assign him or her to one of the Germans from the "reception committee" who had come to obtain free labor. In general, family ties were disregarded, but some of the German administrators allowed exchanges so that married couples, or parents and children, could remain together. This "humane gesture," they explained to the *Kreishauptmann*, would ensure more efficient workers. A few young, good-looking girls were separated from the group and turned over to the German blonde. For what purpose, one could only surmise.

There were still about 250-300 people, men and women, left without assignment. Among them were the secretary and several members of the *Judenrat*, also the doctor—myself—and Mr. and Mrs. S., the parents of the only baby in the ghetto of Grabowiec.

Nobody knew what would happen next. Later, I was told that we would be sent back to Grabowiec and be put to work there. The older people, the sick and the children

would be sent to a special camp, where they would not
have to work and would receive food rations provided by
the German authorities. It would be a kind of "Jewish
reservation."

At about noon the entire operation was finished. Now
came the waiting for the final act: the arrival of the train
that would take the old, the sick and the children too
young for productive work — the human refuse — to their
destination.

It was a long day. The hours seemed to drag on into
eternity. The sun was burning. Some Germans, supposed-
ly "good and sympathetic," gave us bottles of water or
crusts of bread in "fair" exchange for wedding rings,
watches or other jewelry. It became hotter by the hour;
there was not a hint of a breeze.

The people became restless and began to ask questions,
which were answered only by beatings and insults. The
group near the tracks — the children, the sick and the
elderly — were particularly agitated. They had a premoni-
tion of things to come. A question, a request for a drink of
water, or a loud prayer would start a commotion, which
was quelled at once by gendarmes. The sight of bloodied
heads and bleeding mouths with gaps where teeth had
been was the most effective deterrent against unrest, at
least for a while.

The other group, the healthy and the young, was restless also. I was sitting on the ground with that group. We
were still waiting for work assignments. Why did they keep
us waiting so long? What would they do with us?

Mrs. S. approached me. "They put my child over
there," she said, pointing to the "human refuse" standing
near the tracks. "They won't take my baby away from me!
Do you hear me? Get my baby! If you don't get my baby,

you'll be sorry!" She was close to hysteria. "I won't move from here without my baby!" she screamed.

The others tried to calm her, but to no avail. Her screams became louder and louder. "Doctor! Do something! Give her something!" those around her pleaded with me. But there was nothing I could do. I had no drugs in my medical bag. Besides, Mrs. S. would certainly not have taken anything of the sort. But I knew that something would have to be done at once. If things were to get out of hand, the consequences would be unpredictable. The gendarmes nearby had already noticed that something was amiss, and were observing the crowd carefully.

There was only one thing for me to do: cross over to the "human refuse," get Baby S. and bring her back to her mother. Get this baby, the one symbol of Jewish vitality, the one sign that we Jews were not work machines but living creatures with hearts and souls. What other way would there be to demonstrate to the Germans and, more importantly, to myself, that there were still some human feelings left in me as well, that I was still more than a living corpse?

And so, refusing to think of the consequences, I said to Mrs. S., "Don't worry! Don't carry on so! Keep calm! I am going to get your baby! I won't return without her." Everyone, including Mrs. S., was amazed. No one spoke. I myself was shocked when I considered the danger into which I had placed myself and everyone else around me. But it was too late now. I had to keep my promise to Mrs. S.

I got to my feet and stretched my limbs. I was still wearing my overcoat, but I no longer felt the heat. Slowly I moved toward the group near the tracks, the old, the sick and the children, where Baby S. was supposed to be. I purposely stopped near the place where my patient, the chief of the gendarmerie, was standing. I looked at his feet, stood there for a few moments, then deliberately turned away and walked on. The gendarme on guard was flabbergasted. He did not know what all this meant. But he said nothing; he merely gave a smile, so as not to appear stupid. The rest of the gendarmes may have thought that, for some reason, I had just requested, and received, permission from the chief of the gendarmerie to cross over to the other group.

When I reached the group where I expected to find Baby S., I was besieged with questions and complaints. "It's so hot! We're starving! What's going to happen to us? Take us away from here! We'll give you anything you want! Just help us!" I did not reply. What could I have said? Pity, anger, desperation and helplessness made me numb. I felt like a stone, deaf, mute.

I found Baby S. lying on the ground, her skin red from the burning sun. Her soiled diaper had dried out and stuck to her little body as if it had been glued on. The baby was whimpering faintly. I looked around me. So much misery, so much suffering! Why? And I asked myself: Why should I attempt to save this one infant when it meant to risk the lives of so many other human beings, including my own? What future was there in store for this baby? I felt sick, but I had promised to save this child. I was still a human being, I told myself. I had not yet become an animal, looking out only for myself. To finish what I had set out to do now became a test of my self-respect, a proof that I was still a man, not a beast.

I tore holes into the pockets of my overcoat. Then I squatted near the baby's head, put my hands through the holes in my coat pockets and grabbed the child by its arms. I slowly got to my feet, hiding my "contraband" beneath my overcoat. Baby S. stopped whimpering. I felt dizzy for a moment, but quickly returned to my senses and started to walk back toward the other group, where Mrs. S. was waiting.

Meanwhile, a commotion had started among some elderly people near the spot where I had picked up Baby S. One old woman, apparently deaf, was trying to reach the outhouse near the main building of the station. Some of the others called to her to come back, but she did not hear them. One of the gendarmes came and ordered her to return to her group, but she did not understand him. He hit her. She began to whimper and cry. The gendarme, enraged, pulled his gun. At last, the woman realized that she must have done something wrong. She stopped in her tracks and headed back for her group, but it was too late. The crack of the gendarme's revolver and her screams became one, and the woman collapsed at the officer's feet. Before her body could hit the ground, the gendarme bent over and snatched her woolen shawl from her shoulders. By that time I had reached the edge of the group from which I had retrieved Baby S. I had heard the shots, but did not become aware of what had happened until I saw the woman on the ground and the gendarme standing over her, tugging at her shawl.

For an instant, the gendarme's eyes met mine. I do not know what was in my eyes at that moment, but his eyes were large, blue and empty of all emotion, including anger. There was nothing. Only emptiness.

I moved on slowly, my hands in my coat pockets, each hand holding one of the baby's arms under my coat. "Act normally! Don't show any fear!" I told myself. The gendarme and I were still looking at each other steadily. My eyes hurt from my intense efforts not to blink.

Abruptly, the gendarme thrust his gun back into its holster. Then he turned on his heel and quickly walked away. So far, so good, I thought. . . . Or was it? Suddenly I realized that there was a deadly silence all around me. Even the moans of the sick and the hungry had subsided. Nothing seemed to be moving, not even the air. The only sounds I could hear were my own heartbeat and the crunch of the gravel beneath my boots. There was something strange and threatening in this silence. I looked around. I tried to catch someone's eye for a clue, but everyone, master and victims alike, seemed to have turned away from me, pretending that I was not there. From the corner of my eye I saw the German blonde staring at me with wide-open eyes. She started talking to the SS officer with her and pointed at me. I quickly turned my eyes away but I was still able to see the SS man grab the girl's arm and lead her away quickly toward the station building.

My heart beat faster and faster, as if it were racing with itself. Perspiration dripped down my forehead into my eyes so that I could hardly see. I tripped, looked down — and then, all at once, everything became clear to me, deadly clear.

From under my coat two tiny legs were dangling rhythmically, while the soiled diaper, held around the baby's thighs by a safety pin, was dragging on the ground!

I felt sick to my stomach. My head began to spin. Cold, clammy sweat covered my whole body. "Don't stop now! Be calm!" I muttered to myself. "There's nothing you can do now. They've all seen it." But how was I to keep the baby's arms from slipping from my hands? How could I keep my heart from pounding? How could I stop being frightened? "Walk faster!" I told myself. "O God! Help me hold on! Only a little while longer!"

When I reached the group of the young and the healthy on the other side, where Mrs. S. was waiting, I almost fell.

The baby slipped out of my hands into her mother's lap. I did not stop. I kept on walking. I felt all the blood draining from my face. My knees became weak, but I kept on walking until I reached the outhouse. I did not turn my head. I was in a fog. I leaned against the fence and held onto a loose board. Everything was spinning around me. My legs felt like rubber and I slumped to the ground.

Suddenly a strong hand pulled me up, and a slap on my face brought me around. It was my patient, the chief of the gendarmerie. "*Du Schwein!*" he shouted. "You pig! "you could have been killed, when I'm not yet cured."

CHAPTER THREE

The Virgin Mary

I slowly opened my eyes. I was not dreaming. I was still alive. I looked around me. I was half buried in a stack of hay. My whole body shivered. I felt cold. I started to dig myself out of the hay carefully so as not to make too much noise, stopping often, listening to make sure no one was there, that no one could hear or see me. There was a palpable silence all around, broken only by the rustle of the hay. I was glad. No one saw or heard me. That was just fine.

At last I climbed out of the haystack. I stretched my aching limbs and I shook off the hay. It was still dark. I could see nothing, neither the sky overhead nor the ground beneath my feet. I could distinguish only the silhouette of the haystack suspended by some miracle between the sky and the earth in a vast expanse, trying to shake itself free, it seemed, from the morning fog.

No one saw me, no one heard me. So nobody would be looking for me. I was alone. That was good. Or was it? To be alone — at present that was all I wanted. But another aspect of being alone began to penetrate my mind. Alone...all alone in the world. Where was my wife? Where were my parents? But I could not let myself dwell on such thoughts. There were more immediate, pressing problems to solve. This was neither the time nor the place for self-pity. There were important decisions to be made. I was alive. All well and good. But what was I to do next? Where should I go? What about food?

Dawn was rapidly approaching. Now, at last, I realized where I was. I could not remain here any longer. I decided to head back for Grabowiec. I still had my Gentile patients and friends there. Surely, they would help me, perhaps find me a place to hide from the Germans. But supposing they would turn away from me? I vowed that I would not let the Germans catch me alive. This resolve had sustained me for two years, in Stalag IA, at the labor camp in Biala Podlaska, in Grojec and in Warsaw. I decided to keep the promise I had made to myself and remain alive and sane.

This perseverance, this instinct of self-preservation had brought me to the haystack from which I had just extricated myself.

I attempted to make plans for my immediate future, but the events of the last few days kept crowding my brain. I realized that I should block the past from my thinking and concentrate on the future instead. But that was easier said than done. Finally, I decided to put my trust in the old Polish folk saying, "Things always have a way of working out somehow." Judging from my experiences of the two years that had gone before, telling myself that things always had a way of working out seemed a sensible substitute for detailed, involved plans that carried no guarantee of success.

* * *

How had I come to the haystack that I was now so eager to leave behind me?

I remembered the order to assemble on the lawn in front of the Judenrat *headquarters in Grabowiec, the announcement that all the Jews of Grabowiec would be "resettled" in Hrubieszow, where, the SS officer had told us, the Jews would live and work together in a miniature "Jew-*

ish state," protected by the kindly German authorities from the wrath of the local Gentile populace.

The decision what to take with me to Hrubieszow had posed no particular problem. All I had to pack was some underwear and my medical bag. I went to the ladies in the pharmacy and to a few other Gentile friends to bid them farewell. Some of them advised me not to leave with the other Jews but to go into hiding. But I had decided to remain with the Jews of Grabowiec and to share their fate, whatever that would be.

That was why I had risked my life to save Baby S. Whether or not the baby survived the war, I do not know, but I will never forget my feeling of satisfaction at having proven to myself that, despite all the inhumanity I had seen, I had still been capable of performing an act of human kindness.

In Hrubieszow, some of the Jews from Grabowiec headed straight for the homes of relatives and friends; others went to seek temporary shelter at the headquarters of the Judenrat. Rumor had it that we would be assigned permanent housing and even food ration cards the next day. But no one cared to check whether these rumors were based on fact. People were afraid to learn the truth.

I moved in with my friend, Dr. Jacob Feldman, a landsman of mine from Pinsk, who had attended high school with me. Dr. Feldman feared the worst, but then he had always been a pessimist. I tried my best to cheer him up, but I did not believe my own words of encouragement. Deep down I knew: This was not a "resettlement," but one more step toward liquidation.

No one slept that night. We waited—for what?

At about five o'clock the next morning, all the Jews of Hrubieszow, along with the newcomers from Grabowiec, were rounded up by the Polish police, which was aided by the Jewish ghetto police. Our next stop was a square in front of Judenrat headquarters. This time we were not permitted to take anything with us. It took several hours to assemble all the people and find those who had taken refuge in cellars and other hideouts. Children were crying, women were screaming, and the Germans accompanied their commands, as usual, with shouts and brutal beatings. At last, a column was formed and about 6,000 Jews moved in the direction of the railroad station, some distance away from the town. By then I had already marched in similar columns several times before. It had always been the same: tired, frightened people with bundles on their backs and children in their arms, walking, walking—not knowing where and to what end.

At the station, a long line of freight and cattle cars, most of them painted red, as if with blood, was waiting. The column was herded toward the open doors of the cars. We were tired and hungry. Some collapsed on the ground, unable to stand any longer.

Suddenly, as if from out of nowhere, a band of Einsatzgruppen, gendarmes and SS men appeared. Hell broke loose. Screams and shouts in Yiddish, Polish and Ukrainian filled the air, and above it all, the German command, "Raus! Raus!" ("Out! Out!"). Shots rang out, whips cracked, children cried. It was a bizarre, truly satanic symphony. To escape the German whips and rifle butts, the people fairly leaped into the cars. The moans of the injured amidst the constant German shouts, "Raus! Raus! Schneller! Schneller!" ("Out! Out! Faster! Step on it!") added to the horror.

The train was already full, but half the people were still standing on the platform. The Germans seemed to be in a hurry; they began to pack the remaining Jews into the cars, again speeding up the operation with their fists, their sticks and the butts of their rifles. At last, all the human cargo had been squeezed into the cattle cars, like so many sardines. It was impossible to turn around in one's place, impossible even to move.

The car doors clanged shut from the outside. Gradually we realized what the Germans had in store for us. This was the end. It would be just as we had heard over and over again: Whoever survived this journey would die in the gas chambers. We were still alive, but our hell had already begun. The cries of the children mingled with the sobs of the women and the prayers of the men. At last, we could no longer ignore the truth.

Several old people and one child had been trampled in the stampede toward the cars. Some of them died in the cars, on their feet. There was no room for them to fall.

The smells of excrement and sweat were overpowering. People relieved themselves where they stood. In addition, there was the stifling heat. The railroad car was fast turning into a living cemetery!

My friend, Dr. Feldman, and I found ourselves in the same cattle car as Mr. Brandt, the head of the Judenrat of Hrubieszow. Brandt was a very honest, nice elderly gentleman, always immaculately dressed. On this day he had put on his best holiday attire, as if he had been invited to an important event. He had on a new hat, and a gold chain dangled from his vest pocket. An elegant black cane with a monogram completed the outfit.

The train remained in the station for many hours. From time to time, the door of our car was opened and guards gave us water in exchange for cash, watches or jewelry. "Better give all this to us," the guards said. "Where you're going, you won't have any use for that stuff. What you need right now is water, and that we will give you." And so the people gave all their valuables to the guards. In return, they received salt water.

It was getting dark. The heat and the stench in the car became unbearable. Some people vomited on their neighbors.

"Jacob," I said to my friend Dr. Feldman, "as soon as this train pulls out of the station, I'll jump off."

"How d'you expect to do that?" Feldman wanted to know.

"Through the window near the top," I replied.

Feldman looked up and said nothing. He only shook his head. The windows of our car, like those of all freight and cattle cars in Poland, were small and set high on the walls, almost directly under the ceilings. They were just large enough for a man of average size to crawl through. But how would I be able to reach them? I appraised the situation. What were my chances? It was dark, but a little light still filtered through the window. The window and the light represented freedom, perhaps even life. Even if I failed and died while trying to escape, I would have lost nothing. Moreover, my very attempt to escape would prove that I still possessed some self-respect, that I was not yet completely dehumanized and I was not about to walk passively to the slaughter.

But how was I to reach the window?

I decided to confide my intention to the people standing nearest to me. The only way to reach the window would be over the heads of other passengers. My first attempt ended in failure. The crowd was too tightly packed around me. Someone said I should wait until the train had started moving. The rocking of the cars would make it easier for me, and for those who would help me escape, to move.

This made sense. I marveled how anyone could think with such logic even in a situation such as ours.

It was very dark now. A strange silence ensued, disturbed only from time to time by the moans of a child (I think it was the child of my friend Dr. Gelbart from Cracow) and by a half-crazed old man mumbling over and over again the Hebrew words Al het she-hatanu, *the solemn confession of sins recited by Jews on Yom Kippur, the Day of Atonement.*

Suddenly, there was a strident squeak. The locomotive jerked the train forward, stopped, moved backward, then lurched forward once again. People were thrown one way, then back to their original positions. No one fell; the car was too crowded for that. But I did indeed feel a little less confined.

Now the lamentations and screams began in earnest. Sobs of Al het *were joined by cries of* Sh'ma Yisrael— *"Hear O Israel," the supreme confession of faith—and other prayers. This macabre chorus was accompanied by the squeaks of the train wheels on the iron tracks and the mournful whistle of the locomotive. Added to all this, the stench of sweat, urine and excrement filled the car with the fetid atmosphere of death.*

At last the train, having gathered the requisite speed, moved on briskly to its unknown destination. No one wanted to think, but we all knew that this was the train of the doomed. It carried human beings who had been robbed of everything, including their personal dignity, reduced to the level of cattle, and were now being taken to the slaughter. After a while, the cries and lamentations stopped and there was silence once again, except for the rhythmic clickety-clack of the train.

The time for action had come. I asked Jacob Feldman whether he would join me. He refused. After the war, I learned that he lived to arrive at the train's last station: Sobibor. There, he took his own life.

Those few others whom I had initiated into my plan to escape now lifted me up bodily, passing me over the heads of the others to the window, which was screened by barbed wire. I cut my hands tearing off the wire, but I felt no pain. At last I could breathe fresh air. This window was my threshold to the world, to freedom, to life. I had no other desire now but to cross that threshold.

I put my head out the window and looked around. I saw I would be able to squeeze through the window, but I would not be able to jump directly out of the train. I had promised some of the others that if I managed to get to the outside of the car I would open the doors so others could escape also. Consequently, I could not simply jump from the car. I would have to get to the steps directly beneath the doors of the car.

My fellow conspirators were holding me by my legs as I bent halfway out the car window. Every cattle car and freight car had a metal ladder on the outside running from the steps of the door to the roof. If only I could reach that ladder! But how was I to do it?

All at once, I knew. The cane of our most distinguished passenger, Mr. Brandt, the chairman of the Judenrat of Hrubieszow! With most of my body hanging out the window I reached back and grabbed the arched handle of Mr. Brandt's cane. Then, holding the cane by its other end, I pushed it out the window and looped the handle into one of the rungs of the ladder outside, praying all the while that the cane should not slip from my grasp. On a signal, the others who had been holding me by the legs let go of me. My body described an arch as it left the car and hit the side of the ladder, but I still managed to hold on to Mr. Brandt's cane. Within seconds, I had reached the steps of the car door.

My head was spinning from the wind outside, and at the thought of what I had just done. I was now outside the car. I was alive. I could run. I would not be gassed or cremated in an oven! I would not rot in a concentration camp!

I tried the door of the car. It was not locked, and it opened quite easily.

The sight of the door opening and of a Jewish face outside came as a shock to those inside the car who had known nothing of my escape. Some became hysterical. Others, especially the younger ones, began to jump off the train. "Jump in the direction in which the train is moving!" I shouted, but I doubt that they could hear me. People jumped in whichever way they could, just to be out of that stench, that hell.

I do not know how many people made it. The guards in the middle and rear cars of the train became aware of what was happening and began to shoot. "Close that door!" people inside the train shouted at me. "They'll kill us all because of you!" Some of them threatened to push me off the steps. I heard the whistle of bullets around me. No one was jumping now. The machine-gun fire stopped. There were only occasional rifle shots, probably fired at fugitives from the train.

I closed the door, but only partially so that it would still open without difficulty if others decided to jump at some later stage of the journey. Then I looked around. The train was running smoothly on an even terrain. My turn had come. I had experience in jumping from moving vehicles. I had frequently jumped on and off moving trolley cars during my student days.

Here, I had to look out for telephone poles, rocks, and holes in the ground. I took a deep breath, threw myself forward, executed several somersaults and landed safely on the ground. Once again I heard gunfire. I did not move but lay quietly where I had landed, waiting until the train had vanished into the darkness.

I got to my feet. My first act was to reach into my coat pocket where, before leaving Grabowiec, I had put a packet of potassium cyanide—just in case. It was still there. Thank God. I took another deep breath. I had to move on, but where was I to go?

I wanted to get on the highway that linked Hrubieszow with Uchanie, from where I would go on to Grabowiec. I hoped I would be able to walk all night, but my legs felt heavy. They could not carry me any farther. My gait became unsteady. My brain ceased to function. I could not take another step.

It was then that I saw the haystack. I decided to lie down for just a little while—only for a short rest. . . .

* * *

But now it was morning and I could no longer afford the luxury of glorying in my past escapes. I had to get on with the business of securing my future survival.

Soon I was well on my way. I passed the village of Uchanie. In two or three hours I would be in Grabowiec. Luck was with me. I did not see a soul. I moved among bushes and tall grass, on the constant lookout for a dirt road, a path on which I would feel more secure.

Suddenly I heard the clatter of a horse-drawn wagon. Startled, I looked around. It was too late to hide. I stopped, and when the wagon approached, I jumped on. The driver was an elderly Polish peasant. I nonchalantly gave him the time-honored greeting of the Polish countryside, "Praised be Jesus Christ."

"Forever and ever,"the peasant replied.

"What's new?" I asked.

"Eh? Nothing much. They took away all the Jews from our place. Nobody knows where they took them. The ones they caught later, in hiding, they shot, along with the folks that helped them."

I pretended indifference. "Times are bad," I said. "But what can we do?"

After this exchange, we rode on in silence.

The wagon approached a clearing. "You better get off now, Doctor," said the peasant. "Doctor!" So he knew me. "Walk close to the young trees and no one will see you," he said. "Good luck, and God be with you."

I jumped off the wagon and started to run. I hoped the peasant would not denounce me. To be on the safe side, I changed direction. When the wagon was out of sight, I turned again and went toward a cluster of homesteads where I had treated several patients. By that time dusk had set in. It had begun to drizzle.

When I reached the edge of the wood, I looked for a certain thatched white cottage with red window frames. That cottage stood some distance away from the other houses. I had visited it several months earlier to deliver the baby of the owner's wife. Since these were poor peasants, I had not taken any money from them and had even left them some medication. They were nice people. They would remember what I had done for them. Was there a dog? I could not hear any barking. Good! Like a thief, I crept into the barn and from there into the cottage.

An old woman came to the window. I recognized her. She was the peasant's mother. When she saw me she became frightened, as if she had seen a ghost. She crossed herself and muttered something. I could not hear what she was saying, nor did I care. All I saw was the loaf of bread and pitcher of milk on the table. Only then did I realize that I had not eaten in almost three days. The moment I was inside the cottage I grabbed the bread and almost choked on the first bite. I did not notice that the old woman had gone outside. I ate and ate; nothing else mattered.

Suddenly the door was flung open. It was the old woman, white as a sheet. "It's the Germans!" she screamed. "The Germans are in the village! They're looking for Jews!"

The bread and the pitcher fell from my hands. I rushed out of the house as if someone had been chasing me. I could hear gunfire from the village. I found myself in an open field. There was no place to hide. I did not want to return to the farm and endanger the lives of the peasant and his family. For the first time, I felt that my end was near. The Germans would find me and kill me. "Just don't let them find me near this house." I prayed. "Not here! Not near this poor old woman!" I started to run across the field. The shots came closer and closer. Still there was no place to hide, no bushes, no haystacks, not even a heap of manure.

And then I stopped in my tracks. I remembered that on the top of the hill, where picnics were held on warm summer evenings, there would be refuge for me, after all. It was a wayside shrine with a statue of the Virgin Mary holding her baby in her arms. It was already dark. A light fog had set in. My thoughts focused on one thing: how to get to the shrine without being seen. "A little more darkness, just a little more darkness," I prayed as I made my way up the hill.

Two wagons full of gendarmes and Germans were moving toward Grabowiec. I could hear them talking and laughing as they approached the hill. When the wagons drew up in front of the statue, the passengers saw nothing unusual. Only a man with his hands stretched out toward the Holy Mother, as if in silent prayer. The drivers, who were Poles, removed their hats and crossed themselves. I could hear them distinctly. "Holy Mother! Holy Virgin! Pray for us!" I started to perspire profusely. I felt faint but had to remain immobile on my knees before the statue. I prayed for the strength to hold out only a few minutes more, until the wagons had passed.

Some of the Germans in the wagon also removed their caps and crossed themselves.

The drizzle had turned into a light, cold rain. The wagons picked up speed and moved toward the main highway. From there I could see them enter Grabowiec and turn off to a road on the right where there was a Polish estate now administered by the Germans.

CHAPTER FOUR

Boots

Darkness came on quite suddenly. It was raining. It would be a nasty night. I was shivering — partly from the biting cold, partly from the excitement in anticipation of my first "job." The wind blew icy raindrops into my face, forcing me to squint, so that I could see virtually nothing.

A few times I was ready to start out, only to decide to wait a little longer. The later I started, I reasoned, the better my chances of success. The people in the little house would be asleep and the surprise all the greater. I did not know whom I would find in that house. I had selected it because of its location near the edge of the woods. I felt that if I took the people inside by surprise while they were asleep, without their clothes, they would not be able to pursue me if something went wrong. Still, I hesitated, carefully weighing all the pros and cons. To go — or not to go?

It was late at night when I finally made up my mind. This was it. It was now or never. Trembling from hunger, cold and nervousness, but full of determination, I started out toward my objective. I kept looking in all directions, listening to every sound, making sure that nobody would see me. Nothing could go wrong, I reassured myself. I had figured out every detail. Besides, who would be out so late, and on a night like this? Why, the weather wasn't even fit for a dog to be let out! A dog?! I stopped in my tracks. I had not thought of the possibility that there might be a dog in this household. It would start to bark and my entire plan, the element of surprise, would be lost. But, dog or no dog, I decided to take my chances. I made it to a window. There was no barking. No dogs, then. I heaved a sigh of relief. But I made myself a mental note, "In the future, remember, beware of dogs."

I knocked at the window. A weak voice asked, "Who's there?"

"Open up! Quick!" I shouted. After a while an old man appeared at the door. When he saw the shiny, menacing barrel of my huge revolver, he hastily stepped back.

"Who are you? What do you want?"

"Shut up!" I tried to sound as tough as possible — partly to frighten my victim, partly to cover my own fear and lack of experience in the art of banditry. Apparently, I was successful, for the old man was shaking like a leaf.

"Mister, we are old and poor," he whined. "We have nothing. Please go away."

"All I want is some food, a shirt and some underwear," I said.

An old woman appeared and gave me some bread and milk. I ate and drank like an animal, more and more. Quick — quick. The two old people looked on in bewilderment. When there was no more bread left, I grabbed the clean shirt the woman had given me and ordered both of them to turn around. I changed my underwear and shirt, threatening the old couple that they would be shot if they made so much as a move. Afterwards, I helped myself to some cold boiled potatoes from the oven. I ran out of the house into the darkness of the miserable night, leaving the old man and his wife wondering about this strange bandit who had not even asked them to hand over their money.

Back in the safety of the quiet woods I relived the whole adventure and analyzed every aspect of the "job" I had performed. By and large, I was satisfied with my performance. Although I felt there was some room for improvement, I was proud of myself. A new career had opened for me, with new possibilities and new horizons.

To start with, I was no longer helpless and unprotected. Secondly, I no longer had to endanger my Gentile friends with my occasional visits and requests for food and clothing. Now I could obtain all the necessities of life from strangers. I could move to other areas, other places where I was not known. True, I had only six bullets in my gun, but the people I would visit would never know.

Lying under a tree in the forest on the frozen ground, I was almost happy. I kept congratulating myself on my first exploit. I had made it, after all. I was tired, but I was no longer hungry. For the first time in many, many days my stomach was full. And so I fell asleep.

During the next several weeks I engaged in "operations" near Izbica, Krasnystaw, Boncza and other villages in the area. I never took anything but food and old clothing. Soon I became a rather well-known figure around those parts. After a while the people ceased to be afraid of me, though they wondered who this bandit might be who never wanted anything but food and clothes. I myself sometimes wondered about what I was doing.

* * *

I often relived in my memory the incident that had put me in possession of my shiny new revolver. I had almost been killed, but I was grateful for what had happened.

After my escape from the death train, which, as I later learned, took the entire Jewish population of Hrubieszow to the annihilation camp of Sobibor, I settled down in the vicinity of Grabowiec. I spent the days and most of the

71

nights in the woods, in the underbrush. Only once in a while, during a particularly cold or rainy night, I would seek shelter in a deserted shack or barn. Occasionally I would emerge from hiding to visit one of my patients or friends in town.

The local population, Poles and Ukrainians alike, were still friendly toward me. Frequently they left food for me in prearranged places. The owners of the Grabowiec pharmacy helped me the most. Disregarding the danger to themselves, they supplied me regularly with food and pure alcohol, an abundant source of precious calories.

Gradually, however, there came a change for the worse. Several Christian families were executed by the Germans for having given aid and shelter to Jews. I felt that my Gentile friends were beginning to resent me. In addition, the cold weather had set in earlier than usual that year. Yet I had no alternative but to remain in the Grabowiec area. I was afraid of strangers and of unknown territory.

I was a strong-willed man. I was also blessed with a good physique. Some people in my situation would have given up or turned themselves in to the Germans, but not I. I was determined to take my own life rather than be led like an animal to the gas chambers.

But how much could one endure? My nerves began to give way. Also, hunger took its toll. I lost much weight and strength. I tried to preserve as much energy as possible by sitting still for hours. But then the cold forced me to get up, to walk, and to rub my hands.

I tried to make contact with other fugitives — Poles, Jews, and escaped Russian POWs who were hiding out in the woods — but my efforts ended in failure. Through my Gentile friends I tried to interest some of the Polish underground groups in my services as a fighter and medico.

But it seemed that there were none active in that area, or perhaps it simply was that none of these groups wanted any Jews.

One night, a particularly cold night, I set out for a friendly village. Suddenly, I noticed a cigarette light flickering in the distance. Friend or foe? I could not take any chances. I kept on running until I reached a cluster of thick bushes. Dogs started to bark. I could hear my heart pounding. I checked the little packet of potassium cyanide I had been carrying in my pocket for the eventuality that the Germans caught me. I would not allow them to take me alive.

Something seemed to be happening in Grabowiec. But what was it? Gradually, the noise subsided and silence, broken only by the patter of frozen rain, engulfed the forest. Later, I learned that a group of armed men had raided the village, taking food and other supplies from the peasants. These armed bands were the very people I was so eager to join.

For the next few days I did not leave my hiding place. I did not want to risk being seen by anybody. For two days, I had nothing to eat, and lived only on small sips from a bottle of alcohol the ladies of the pharmacy in Grabowiec had given me. But this alcohol, too, was almost gone. What would I do when there was no more alcohol left? I tried not to think about that. Worrying never helped; besides, one dies only once. I became resigned to my fate. It seemed to me that I had reached the limits of my endurance.

Another day passed, another night spent alone in the woods. I was cold and hungry, almost beyond the point of feeling hunger. I had come to a stage where I no longer sensed hunger but only visualized it. I had begun to daydream about food. Suddenly, a scene from an old Charlie

Chaplin movie, "Gold Rush," the scene where Chaplin ate shoe laces and his partner imagined Chaplin was a turkey, kept gliding into my mind. I tried to sleep but I was tormented by dreams about food — food and warmth. The nights were the worst — the dreams, the cold and the silence.

That morning which has remained in my memory began with a dense fog and biting frost. I woke up shivering. I did not feel hungry, only empty inside, shaky and very cold.

I took inventory of my possessions: one jacket, one short overcoat, one pair of pants and — one pair of boots. These boots on my feet were the most important, the most precious of my possessions. Without my boots, I might as well have been dead. I could, perhaps, have obtained an additional old jacket or even some rags from friendly peasants, or steal them if need be. But boots could never be replaced, and without boots I knew I would simply freeze to death.

My boots were practically new. They were elegant officer's boots, made to order. To me, they represented one thing only: survival. With them on my feet, I felt well-dressed. If only I could manage to get some food! I had not eaten in three or four days. In one of my coat pockets there was the bottle that once had been full of alcohol, 96 per cent proof, loaded with calories. I would drink one gulp daily, sometimes two, but the bottle was not bottomless. There now remained perhaps one or two swallows of the precious liquid, just enough for one more day. What was I to do? Drink it up all at once, or subdivide it into smaller rations? It seems incredible that in the mind of an educated, intelligent grown-up man such a problem should have assumed earth-shaking proportions — into a veritable

Shakespearean "To be or not to be." Drink it all at once, or perhaps save it indefinitely? It is beyond belief that a little alcohol should require so much mental stress and momentous decision-making. I was fully aware of the tragic-comical situation, but I was very hungry, very cold, very weak and very much alone.

I weighed all the arguments for and against each choice. Should I drink it all now? If I drank up the last of my alcohol today, what would happen tomorrow? It seemed more logical to stretch the calories, but oh, the emptiness, the hunger pain! On the other hand, I might find some food during the night. I might be able to visit a friend in the village. Also, I might be dead by tomorrow. If any of these eventualities materialized, the alcohol would be wasted altogether. And so I made my decision. I opened the bottle, put it to my lips, poured all its contents into my mouth and swallowed the liquid in one gulp. But apparently it had been too much to swallow all at once, for when the liquid went down my gullet I felt severe pain, probably due to the sudden stretching of the gullet, in addition to the burning sensation caused by the alcohol.

However, the pain slowly subsided and I began to feel better. Warmth spread over my entire body. I even felt stronger. Also, the sun broke through the fog. It would be a nice day. All this, and the effect of the alcohol on my mood, made me see my situation in brighter colors. A sense of well-being enveloped me. Once again, I began to daydream about food, a cozy home and a warm bed.

When the sun hid behind a cloud, I felt a little chilly again. I got to my feet and started to walk. Exercise would do me good, I thought. I rubbed my stiff hands and began to dance — first in one place and then in circles, to get warm, to get in shape.

Suddenly, I heard a noise behind me. I stopped dancing, turned around, and froze. In front of me, about ten or fifteen feet away, stood a man. He was tall and well-built. He was dressed in a short, fur-lined overcoat, ear muffs and a pair of good sturdy boots.

We looked at one another appraisingly. By that time I knew many people in the area, but I've never seen this man before. Who was he? What was he doing here?

Finally, he spoke. "I am from the *Kripo*," he said in a clumsy Polish. "Who are you and what are you doing in the woods?"

"Me? Oh — I'm just dancing, that's all," I replied. I was so stunned that I could think of no better answer than to describe what I had been doing when he had first appeared.

It must have sounded rather amusing, because the stranger actually smiled. "Not to worry," he said. "I'm not really a policeman. We're in the same boat, you and I. We're both hiding from the Germans. They're in the next village now, rounding up young men and women for forced labor in Germany. I got away and so here I am. Don't be afraid."

By that time I had regained my composure and was no longer frightened. The stranger's story sounded credible. He became quite talkative. Now he said that he was, in fact, a Russian soldier. He had been a POW but had escaped from the prison camp. His native village in the Ukraine had been destroyed and his parents killed. He had been hiding out in the area for several months now and had made friends. He offered me a cigarette and even rolled the tobacco for me. Gradually, my suspicions vanished and I was completely at ease. So, when my feet began to freeze again, I resumed my dancing.

I had my back to the stranger when, suddenly, I heard the command, "Hands up and turn around! Slowly!" I had no choice but to do as I was told. I found myself looking into the barrel of a large automatic revolver. Gone were the friendly voice and the sympathetic attitude of the stranger.

So, all his sob story had been only an act! At that moment I felt no fear, only contempt and rage. "You die only once, I said to myself, and now my time had come. I waited for the shot, but there was none. Instead, the stranger said, "Take off your overcoat! Slowly! Let it drop from your arms!" Mechanically, showing no emotions, I obeyed. Now, at last, I understood: this stranger was an ordinary highwayman, and I was about to be robbed!

"Take off your jacket, undo your belt and let your pants drop!" My overcoat and jacket were still in fairly good condition, but the pants? They were old and torn. What would anyone want with them? Then it came to me: no man could run with his pants down. Yes — that made sense. Next, I was ordered to take off the tatters that once had been my shirt. A thousand thoughts raced through my head. The situation was tragic but at the same time grotesque. Here I was, a full-grown man, with my pants and underwear resting on my boots, cold, hungry, furious at the humiliation of it all and, even worse, helpless, held up at gunpoint by another man as strong and healthy as I was.

I did not know how long I remained in that position. It seemed a lifetime. Then another order. "Pick up your pants! Fasten your belt!" I eagerly obeyed. The stranger had me covered all the time. What will happen to me next? I wondered. If he is a policeman after all, why doesn't he kill me? What does he want to do with me?

My question was promptly answered by his next command. "Let me have your boots! They're much too good for the likes of you!"

The words penetrated deep into my brain. "My boots? Oh, no! I won't part with my boots! I'll never give away my boots to anybody!" You could always find rags, beg for them or steal them, to cover your body, but you could never replace boots, and without boots, you were dead. If this man wanted my boots, he would have to shoot me first. Without boots, especially in the winter, I would never survive.

A change came over me. My bewilderment, fright, helplessness and self-pity all left me. I would put up a fight. My entire being feverishly prepared to do battle. But how? If only I could come closer to my assailant, I would attack him. The element of surprise would be in my favor, since the man probably did not expect a fight. Anyway, this was my only chance. If I failed, I would at least have died like a man.

I tried to appear calm while I pretended, standing on one leg, to pull off one of my boots. I couldn't do it. I tried once more and at the same time hopped on the other leg, moving a little closer to my attacker.

"Hurry up. I don't have all day!" he said.

"I'm doing my best," I retorted angrily, "You try taking off your boots standing on one leg. Especially when they haven't been off your feet in weeks."

The man seemed to understand. "All right. Go on! You talk too much!" he said. I tried again and again, hopping on my other leg to gain another few inches. The man was relaxed, sure of himself and also of his victim's helplessness, so sure that he did not notice my maneuvering to come closer to him.

I looked around, judging the distance that still remained between him and me. I put my leg down, bent forward, then raised my other leg. But instead of grabbing it with my hand, as if to remove the boot, I stretched my knee and with all the might I could muster, I landed the tip of my boot on my assailant's chin. The blow was so intense and the surprise so total that the man lost his balance. Another blow sent him falling to the ground. The gun fell out of his hand and I grabbed it before my opponent could get back to his feet.

Now the roles had been reversed. The victim had become the master. I was very excited, but I did not know exactly what to do next. The man was begging for mercy. He started talking in a good Russian. He hadn't intended to harm me, he said. He had told me to take off my pants only because he wanted to find out whether I was Jewish (to see whether I had been circumcised). He had not intended to rob me. After all, he himself was hiding out from the Germans. In fact, he suggested that we team up. Life would then be easier for both of us.

I was too excited to listen to him. All I could think about was how to convince this bandit, and myself, that I was not afraid and that I was tough. "Shut, up, you son of a bitch!" I shouted, adding a few obscenities to appear even tougher.

I ordered my captive to take off his overcoat and jacket, and to let his pants down. Telling him to let his pants down turned out to be a grave mistake, for when the man started to unfasten his belt buckle, he produced a hand grenade that had been hidden under the belt, and threw it at me.

We both hit the ground at the same time. The roar of the explosion tore the air. Its effect was magnified by the echoes and by the noise from the frightened animals in the woods.

Each of us ran off in opposite directions, fearing to turn around, afraid of each other. But now I had a gun!

I knew I had to get far away from that spot as quickly as possible because the Germans might have heard the explosion and would come running.

I did not dare to look behind me until I had reached the edge of the woods. Seeing no one in pursuit, I rushed through an open field to another wooded area where I finally sat down, physically and mentally exhausted by the events of the day.

Only then did I realize that I was limping and that my left wrist hurt me very badly. My left leg also hurt. I had been injured by pieces of shrapnel from the hand grenade. I made an improvised dressing from pieces of my shirt and dismissed my injuries as a minor incident in an otherwise magnificent day. I was happy. I was armed! At last, I had a gun!

CHAPTER FIVE

The
Witch Doctor

At first, I thought that the injuries to my wrist and leg were only superficial. But a few days after my encounter with the bandit, I developed a high fever, chills and also severe pain, especially in my wrist.

Only then did I realize that I had suffered a compound fracture of my forearm, which needed immediate attention. I decided to visit one of my patients, a peasant in the village of Czechowka near Grabowiec, who was also my friend. He allowed me to stay in his barn for two days. He managed to get me some plaster and bandages. I myself then applied a cast to my wrist. Eventually, the fracture healed. But a fragment of shrapnel still remained. It was removed in 1944 by my friend and classmate, Dr. Lukasic.

I returned to the woods and resumed my search for contacts with organized resistance groups. After a while I was introduced to a man, allegedly an officer in a local unit of the newly-organized underground army. He said he was interested in having me join his unit; they needed every man willing and able to fight the Germans. A doctor would come in especially handy. But, he added, not just yet. They would call me when the time was ripe. If fighters were needed so badly, I wondered, why didn't he accept me immediately? The answer was clear. I had one strike against me: I was Jewish and many Polish underground units did not want Jews.

During the day I roamed the woods, sleeping either outdoors, or, if the weather was very cold or bad, in an isolated barn. I knew that there were armed groups of Russians who had escaped from POW camps, and also armed Polish Gentiles who had been forced to flee from their homes and hide out in the woods. I hoped to locate such a group. However, a Jew had to be very careful not to fall into the hands of the so-called "National Armed Forces." These were Polish Fascists who hated Hitler but shared his ideas about the Jews. They frequently helped turn Jews over to the Germans and, in some instances, killed Jews on their own.

At last, one day, my dream came true. In the woods, near Chelm, I met a group of Poles and Russians. When I first saw them following me, armed to the teeth, I turned tail and ran. They stopped me and tried to interrogate me. They thought I was a German or a collaborator. My fluent Russian probably saved my life. I was promptly accepted into their unit.

However, my new comrades in arms looked at me with some suspicion. I was a doctor. They did not seem to have much use for professional men; also, they did not really trust Jews. And how, they wondered, had I obtained my revolver?

But within a few days the ice was broken and I became a full-fledged "bandiore," as the group was called. In fact, I was elected a group leader. My particular group consisted of eight poorly-armed Poles and Russians. We shared among us seven Polish carbines and my own heavy "Vis" revolver that I had acquired from the bandit in the woods.

My unit, like other similar groups in the woods, did not have any ideological incentive to fight and die. They had not risked their lives to escape from prison camps only to die in battle. Their aim was simply to survive until the end of the war.

In the beginning, the local populace had been sympathetic to them, but in time, when the "bandiores," calling themselves "partisan fighters," started to rob people, get drunk and become involved with local women, the relationship grew less amicable. Another reason for the growing coolness of the peasantry toward the "bandiores" was that the Germans regarded helping "bandits" in any way as a grave crime, for which the guilty party would be executed with his entire family.

As the leader of my group, I started a campaign for transforming the unit into an effective force of partisan fighters. With the authority of my position and also because I was the oldest among them and well-educated, I was able in time to explain to my men what our aims should be. Our first priority, I said, was not to antagonize the local populace; the second was to fight the Germans and their fellow travelers. We should obtain food, clothing and arms from the Germans. Whatever we could not use we should either destroy or give away to the peasants.

I must have been very persuasive, because my men agreed with me. Our ranks were soon augmented by the addition of two more armed Polish recruits. In the middle of December, 1942, we performed our first mission. We ambushed a German military vehicle.

For our first operation we selected a not too frequently traveled road between Mionchin and Hrubieszow, a road with which I was familiar. Since we did not know when a German military vehicle would pass our way, we kept vigil at the road almost every night for almost a week — with no luck. We spent the daytime mostly in the woods. At night we took up stations on both sides of the road and waited. My orders were that, when I gave the signal, we were to open fire with everything we had. After a few days, people got impatient and started to grumble, but finally, one night we saw the headlights of an approaching car. When the car came close I gave the signal and we opened fire. We succeeded in shooting out the car's headlights and the car started to skid and swerve in all directions. Finally it went off an embankment and turned over. We cautiously approached the wrecked car. The passengers, a German lieutenant and two enlisted men, were dead. In the wreckage we found a small seventy-five bullet machine gun and two carbines, plus a generous supply of ammunition. There was also a large supply of cigarettes and several bottles of alcohol. We burned the car and then quickly left the site of our ambush, elated at our initial success.

Next, we moved into another area, a forest near Krasnystaw. There we spent the day evaluating the results of our "operation" on the Mionchin-Hrubieszow road. That evening, we made our way to a small settlement, where we bought food, paying for it with cigarettes and alcohol. The people to whom we spoke seemed nervous. When we wanted to know the reason for their apprehension, they told us that during the preceding night there had been a big battle between Germans and "parachutists" on the road between Mionchin and Hrubieszow. In that encounter, many German military vehicles had been destroyed and many Germans killed.

The following night we met people who claimed that an entire panzer division had been annihilated by the parachutists during that battle. There were various theories about the identity of the parachutists, but no one knew for sure from where the parachutists had come.

It seemed that the farther away we moved from the site of our ambush, the more lurid the reports became about the fierceness of the battle and the extent of the German losses.

86

My men listened to the reports of the fighting and relished the importance they had suddenly assumed. But there were some who felt they already had enough of the fighting.

Most of the boys from the area returned to their homes. Some of the Russian POWs left in search of larger Russian partisan units that were moving east, trying to reach the woods and swamps of Polesie. The remainder of our group roamed the villages and woods in the vicinity of Chelm, Hrubieszow, Krasnystaw and Zamosc.

* * *

During the weeks that followed, we carried out several sabotage operations, mainly destroying German property, cutting telephone lines and setting fire to German warehouses. We frequently engaged in skirmishes with the "Blue Police," the Polish police in the service of the Germans, so named because of their blue uniforms.

In addition to ourselves there were other "wild groups" active in the same region, also engaged in sabotage. Together, we inflicted great damage. This provoked German reprisals, directed primarily against the local population. Although the Germans avoided the woods, they nevertheless organized hunts for partisans with frequent sorties into the woods, causing huge losses to themselves, and some casualties among partisans and civilians as well.

Because we lacked a centrally organized leadership and intelligence in our region, the Germans succeeded in dispersing and even annihilating several groups of partisans, thus achieving a temporary lull in resistance, with no major interference from the underground.

* * *

As far as our group was concerned, this lull lasted for about three months. In the meantime, the composition of our unit changed completely. From the original group, only two had remained; the rest either had been killed, or had simply quit. There was also a small influx of new recruits.

Aside from being a "bandiore," I also "practiced" medicine. As a matter of fact, that is how I acquired my nickname, *Znachor*,* or "Witch Doctor."

One very cold night in January or February, 1943, our group raided an isolated farmhouse. We left one of our men to stand guard outside the farm, and I looked over the inside to make sure no one could leave the premises and report us to the Germans. The kitchen and a small alcove were empty. So was the main room, but when I tried to enter the bedroom, the peasant objected, "My wife is very sick. Please do not frighten her."

I hesitated, but my suspicious nature caused me to enter the room despite all of our host's protestations.

When I opened the door, there really was a woman in bed. One could see that she was sick and had a high fever.

I still had in my medical bag a small stethoscope that my good friend and classmate, Dr. Stephanie Mesh, had given me in Warsaw. I examined the sick woman. It turned out that she had a right-side lobar pneumonia. I wrote out, on a scrap of paper, a prescription for a cough syrup. I also showed how prescient I was. Until the appearance of antibiotics, the course of any case of pneumonia — if the patient survived the crisis — could be predicted with accuracy. The patient would run a very high fever, which would fall abruptly from 104 or 105 degrees to normal, usually on an uneven day (the fifth, the seventh or the ninth) after the onset of the illness. Since this woman had already been sick for five days, I was able to tell her family

* Pronounced *ZNA'khor.*

that she would recover on the day following the last sharp rise in her fever.

When my prediction came true and the woman recovered, my grateful patient and her family spread the word that there is among the "bandiores" a *Znachor*, a "witch doctor." When our men visited this family again several weeks later, we were treated with respect, given a good meal and even changes in underwear. We spent half the night at this homestead and, while we were there, I examined a few other neighbors with various less serious but nonetheless bothersome medical problems.

And so the by-name *Znachor* stuck to me and became the underground name by which I was known even long after the war had ended.

* * *

As I mentioned before, civilians giving aid to partisans did so at the risk of severe punishment.

The German authorities had set up a so-called *Kontingent*, or quota system, under which every peasant had to deliver all the milk from his farm to central dairy plants where the cream would be centrifuged and taken away by the Germans. A greater part of the grain and eggs also had to be given to the Germans. In order to have control over the livestock, the Germans tagged every farm animal with an earring. Failure to deliver the assigned quota or to account for every animal in one's possession was a capital offense. It was therefore only natural that whenever partisans "confiscated" part of a peasant's quota and thus endangered the entire village, the resentment of the populace toward the partisans should intensify.

In order to protect the peasants from punishment for failure to fill their quotas, we began to hand out "receipts" for all the produce and livestock we "confiscated" from them. We also threatened that if harm came to any of the peasants, there would be reprisals against the Germans and against the *Volksdeutsche* who had been brought over from German-occupied Russian territory to settle in this highly fertile region in order to "Germanize" it.

I do not know whether these measures caused any change in the German method of dealing with "delinquent" peasants or whether our "receipts" were really "honored" by the German authorities, but it seemed to us that the German punishments became less severe and were gradually discontinued.

In May, 1943, I met a group of partisans under the leadership of Konstanty Mastelarz, better known by his underground name, "The Old One." I had heard about him and his men, but our paths had never crossed before.

"The Old One" was a man in his late fifties. In 1941, the Germans had come to arrest him, but he had not been at home. So they set fire to his farm and killed his wife and only son. Mastelarz took to the woods and began to fight back. His group was one of the first to join the newly-organized "People's Army." I joined his unit.

At about the same time, a group of Russians, under the command of a man known by the underground name of "Grishka" operated in the same area. Initially, they engaged in the same operations against the Germans as we did, but later this group became demoralized and, instead of fighting the Germans, took the less dangerous route of merely struggling for survival. Numerous attempts by "The Old One" and myself to transform these individuals into a fighting unit failed, but we kept in touch with them and, on occasion, they would cooperate with us in larger operations against the enemy.

By that time, our own partisan group had grown and was able to enlarge the scope and area of our activities. We cut telephone wires, destroyed regional administrative offices, burned official documents and "confiscated" useful materials. We raided German and Polish police stations. Our biggest battle took place in September, 1943, in Surhow, near Chelm. In this encounter we killed ten Germans; we lost four of our men.

By October, 1943, the damage caused by underground activities reached such proportions that the Germans were forced to take action. Despite their fear of the woods, they again launched manhunts for the "bandits," as they called us. They paid dearly for this offensive, but they succeeded in clearing some of the woods of partisan units. "The Old One," myself and five others from our group kept together and survived the manhunts. We were tired, hungry and ill-equipped, and we had lost several men. Our situation was desperate. From local people we found out that "Grishka" and his men had been cornered in the Boncza woods. We could do nothing to take the pressure off them. Yet, we felt we had to help them somehow. But what was to be done?

"Panska Dolina" near Zamosc was a large Polish estate that had been seized from its rightful owners by the Germans. Talking to the neighboring villagers we found out that four or five soldiers and one high-ranking German officer were stationed there. We also learned that there were no guards outside at night and no dogs. I thought it would be a great boost to our morale and a spectacular achievement if we would be able to occupy this property. "The Old One" hesitated, but I finally succeeded in convincing him that it could be done. The others saw the danger but reluctantly went along with my plan.

The weather that day was miserable. A cold drizzle added to the general discomfort. Night was rapidly approaching. It became very dark. I stationed one man at each corner of the estate, about 200 feet from the main building. Each of the men was supposed to pretend that he had a whole unit of partisans behind him. I instructed them to remain quiet until I would give them a signal. Then they were to rush toward the house, making a lot of noise, talking aloud to themselves and, in general, creating the impression that the house was surrounded by dozens of partisan fighters. If the Germans opened fire on us, "The Old One" would take whatever action he considered appropriate.

I left my machine gun with "The Old One," keeping only one small Browning for myself. I quickly moved toward the main building. The shutters were closed, but I could hear people talking inside, in German.

I knocked on the door, entered and announced, "I am a partisan. I'm just an ordinary soldier, but I speak German. Don't do anything foolish. You are surrounded. You may kill me, but then you'll all die. So, listen to me." The reply was utter silence.

"I want your commander to come out with his weapons on his shoulders," I commanded. "The rest of you will deposit your arms on the table in this room. If you cooperate, no one will be harmed. You have one minute to consider my ultimatum."

For a while, there was silence. Then the answer came. "We will not try to defend ourselves. We'll come out." I said that only the leader was to come out. As I stood waiting at the door, a *Wehrmacht* captain emerged with a machine gun over his shoulders and his hands raised. He stretched out his hand to shake mine. I also extended my hand, reaching not for his hand but for his machine gun. I frisked him to make sure that he had no other weapons concealed about his body. By that time, "The Old One," who had followed me, had arrived at the house. I told him to watch the captain. Meanwhile, I entered the room, where two German soldiers and policemen were standing against the wall, their weapons deposited on the table as I had ordered.

From the door, I told "The Old One" to call on "one man from each partisan group" to enter the building. I wanted our prisoners to think that there were indeed many other fighters nearby. Our men immediately put on a great show of activity. One of them hitched up the wagon in which we had come, while others searched the house and the people inside. We opened a safe and "confiscated" a substantial amount of cash. Besides food and cash, our loot included four rifles, one machine gun, one revolver and eight or nine hand grenades.

In the midst of all this to do, I had an interesting conversation with our unwilling host, the *Wehrmacht* captain. "You know you can't win," he told me. "You don't have any weapons."

"We get our weapons from Germans like yourself," I replied.

"Are you going to kill us?" the captain wanted to know.

"I will not," I answered. "I gave you my word of honor as a partisan, which is sacred, not like the empty promises of a German," I retorted.

We spent no more than about forty minutes at "Panska Dolina." The men piled our wagon high with everything we could put to use, including two slaughtered pigs. When we were ready to go, I handed the captain a written receipt for his weapons and other equipment and authenticated the document with my signature, *"Znachor."* Then we left in a hurry, making a lot of noise in order to give the impression that there were at least sixty of us, not just six. We headed for Zamosc but soon turned around in the direction of Krasnystaw. We unloaded the wagon and left it behind, knowing that the horses would eventually find their way back to "Panska Dolina" by themselves. Whatever meat and other supplies we could not use we gave to the peasants in the area.

The repercussions of this operation were spectacular. The Germans withdrew their forces from Boncza and started a manhunt for *Znachor* and his men. We returned to Boncza. Two weeks later we used similar tactics to disarm two German soldiers on another German-administered farm.

Left to right: Jan Czechowicz, Kotek-Agroszewski, Jim-Czyzewski, Rola-Zymierski, Grab, Temchin, Szot, Cien

Standing left to right: Zbyszek, Grab, Rola-Zymierski, Szot, Temchin, Jim

Liberation of Warsaw, January 17, 1945

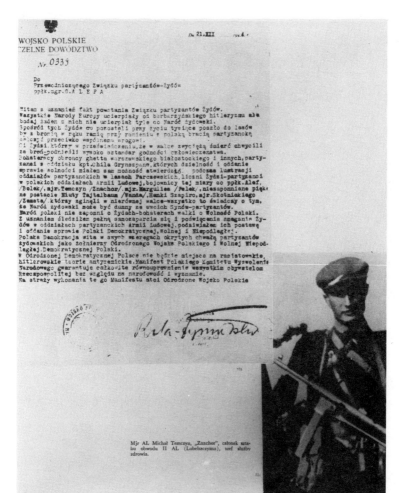

Mjr AL Michał Temczyn, „Znachor", członek szta-
bu obwodu II AL (Lubelszczyzna), szef służby
zdrowia.

To The Union of Jewish Partisans

Thousands of the remaining Jews fled to the forests where, arms in hand, they did battle with the common enemy, shoulder to shoulder with their fellow partisans. These were the heroic defenders of the ghettos of Warsaw, Bialystok and other cities. They were partisans of the division commanded by "Chil" Grynszpan, whose devotion and value to the cause of freedom I personally witnessed during my inspection of the partisan groups. The number of Jewish partisans in the cadres of the People's Army, fighters of the caliber of Lieutenant Colonel Alef (Bolek), Major Temczyn (Znachor), Major Margulies (Felek), and the unforgettably luminous personalities of Niuta Teitelbaum (Wanda), Major Skotnicki (Zemsta), and Hanka Szapiro, who died fighting against overwhelming odds, all testify to the fact that the Jewish Nation may well be proud of its partisan sons.

Rola-Zymierski

Dr. Temchin and his family: Jack, Mira, Shelley

Dr. Emil Sommerstein (1883–1957)

Dr. Michael Temchin (1977)

CHAPTER SIX

A Medical
Consultation

The fall of 1943 and the winter of 1944 were very difficult times for the partisans. In addition to the bad weather, we were plagued by frequent manhunts in the woods. We had to be constantly on the move. At the same time, however, the woods of the Lublin region swarmed with groups of partisans, old and new. This was also the time when groups of similar ideologies and political inclinations combined to form three major underground armies:

1. The *Armia Ludowa* (AL), or "People's Army," was the military arm of progressive parties such as the Socialists, the Communists, the Peasants' party, and various liberal splinter groups and individuals.

2. The *Armia Krajowa* (AK), or "Home Army," represented the philosophy of the Polish government-in-exile in London. The AK was a large organization, active mostly in urban areas, but less so in the countryside. The AK claimed to be liberal, but it was not so liberal when it came to Jews. The AK did not accept Jews too eagerly. Those few Jews who were accepted into the AK mostly did not look Jewish and deliberately used Polish-sounding names. Many of these men perished without revealing their Jewish identity; others survived under their assumed Polish names. As a result, their acts of valor are not recorded where they should be: in the annals of Jewish heroism.

3. The *NSZ*, or "National Armed Forces," represented the Polish variant of Fascism in its ugliest form. They were violently anti-Socialist, and zoologically anti-Semitic, so

much so that they killed any Jews they encountered or else reported them to the Germans.

The antagonism between the progressive AL and the Fascist NSZ was so fierce that we now had to watch out for two enemies: the Germans and the NSZ, and it was difficult to say which one was the more dangerous.

AL units were frequently ambushed by the NSZ and many good men were killed in these fratricidal encounters. The most notorious massacre took place in the village of Borow in the fall of 1943, when about forty AL men were brutally murdered by the NSZ. The NSZ also killed other outstanding AL leaders such as Captain "Grzybowski," "Blyskawica" Andrzej, and many less-known AL fighters.

At the same time, new partisan units — Jewish, non-Jewish and mixed groups — had formed in the woods. The best known among the Jewish units were those led by Chil Grynszpan, Samuel ("Mietek") Gruber, and others. They operated mostly in the Parczew and Janowski woods. In addition to fighting the Germans they also gave protection to Jews in hiding. Late in the spring of 1944 a group of partisans came to our area from the Soviet zone, on the other side of the River Bug. These men were led by a Jewish veterinarian, Dr. Skotnicki, better known by his underground name "Zemsta"(Revenge). He eventually lost his life in a battle with overwhelming German forces. Still later, a Jew named Kasman, whose underground name was "Janowski," commanded a huge unit in the Janowski and Lipskie woods. Also in the spring of 1944, "Bolek" (his real name was Gustaw Alef), a lawyer from Bialystok, organized an AL propaganda and fighting unit that operated in our area.

Our own group also underwent changes. First, we had grown enormously in size. Many young Poles now filled our ranks. Secondly, we had become well known, especially after our exploits at "Panska Dolina" and in Bukowina. We attracted the attention of AL headquarters in the village of Rzeczyca, near Krasnik, where most of the inhabitants sympathized with the partisans, served as couriers and lookouts for the fighters, and provided hideouts for them.

Because of these favorable conditions, the most active and best organized units operated from our area. The Lublin district of the AL had connections with the national underground leadership in Warsaw, which in turn was in contact with the Union of Polish Patriots in the Soviet Union. It was the UPP that kept the AL supplied with literature, communications equipment and weapons dropped by parachute from Soviet planes. But we obtained most of our weapons from direct combat with the enemy.

Until the late fall of 1943, my own role was strictly that of a fighter. Unfortunately, in all our encounters with the enemy there were few wounded. Most of our casualties were those killed. Also, my medical supplies were so meager that all I could do was bandage wounds. Beyond that, my medical knowledge was of little use in the woods.

At this point I must give credit again to the ladies of the pharmacy in Grabowiec, who sent me as many pharmacy items as they could.

Meanwhile, the underground activities of the AL had increased tremendously. There were almost daily encounters with the Germans or the Polish "Blue Police," with heavy loss of life and many wounded. It became clear to me that I could be of a greater value at the headquarters of our Lublin district than in a strictly circumscribed radius of activity.

Early in December, 1943, a group of partisans from the Lublin district, under the leadership of "Przepiorka" ("The Quail"), "Kot" ("The Cat"), Szot and Waclaw

"Jim" Czyzewski eventually became a general in the Polish army and is now retired — turned up in Boncza. Their task was to consolidate all the smaller partisan groups of the region into one unified command, to prevail upon me to join the central organization of AL, and to convince "Grishka" and his boys to join the AL. The effort to enlist "Grishka" and his boys into the AL failed. "Grishka's" group survived the war without fighting. They spent most of the war roaming around Boncza. When the Russians came, these men were absorbed into the regular army, but "Grishka" was court-martialed and shot for having refused to fight as a partisan during the war.

As for me, I was eager to go where the action was. Our unit which I had helped organize gave me an emotional farewell party, and the following night five others and I left the Boncza woods.

The night was cold. After a short, brisk walk, we reached a lumber mill in the village of Wilka. There, we "confiscated" a pair of horses and a wagon. We also destroyed some important machinery. The administrator of the mill, a Pole, treated us to a good supper. We were about to finish eating when the sentry we had posted outside rushed in to tell us that a car was coming toward the lumber mill.

We interrupted our meal and took up stations for an ambush. We approached the car with caution. It took only one burst of fire from our automatics to stop the vehicle. I heard someone ask for help in German. We removed two German noncommissioned officers from the car. They begged for mercy, claiming that they were not Germans but Austrians, who had been forcibly inducted into the *Wehrmacht*. We believed their story. One of the two had been wounded in the head and in both hands. The other had only a superficial leg injury. I used the emergency first aid kit every German soldier carried on his person to treat both men. After removing our loot — two light machine guns, ammunition, cigarettes, vodka and some cash — we set fire to the car. We then went back inside the lumber mill and finished our supper. Afterwards, we continued the journey to our destination, traveling all that night. We spent the next day at a farm not too far from the woods. We took turns patrolling the farm. When it got dark outside we thanked the peasant for his hospitality and continued on our way until we reached Rzeczyca, the "capital" of the AL.

After removing our loot from the wagon, we left the horses we had acquired at the lumber mill, trusting that they would find their way back to the mill on their own.

Rzeczyca was a large village, one of the largest I had ever seen. Its main street was about three miles long. The village was subdivided into three distinct communities: Rzeczyca Ksiazeca, Rzeczyca Panska and Rzeczyca Chlopska. This division was not only geographical but also political. The community of Panska was not actually involved in political activity. The central community, Rzeczyca Chlopska, was a staunch AL stronghold. Rzeczyca Ksiazeca, on the other hand, was a bastion of hostility, hatred and bigotry, the nerve center of the NSZ for the Lublin region. It was very dangerous for someone from our sector of Rzeczyca to enter Rzeczyca Ksiazeca. Our territory included also a somewhat smaller village, Trzydnik, which was populated mostly by a family named Szymanski, which included a host of cousins and other kinfolk.

The Szymanskis were very active in the underground. Many of them had been leftist political leaders before the war. During the war, this family supplied a very large contingent of partisan fighters and leaders. They also suffered a great number of casualties in dead and maimed.

In Rzeczyca Chlopska, the actual meeting place for AL leaders, couriers and agents was a cooperative store run by an agent of ours, Mrs. Momat, whose nickname was "Kuma."

The Germans were aware of what was going on in Rzeczyca. However, they tolerated the situation, since they realized that the pacification of this village would be very costly in arms and manpower. Also, I assume that the destruction of the village would have deprived them of a listening post, since they probably had their spies there. As a consequence, there were never any manhunts for partisans in Rzeczyca.

The day I arrived in Rzeczyca, I treated several patients, mostly individuals with neglected wounds. I was also taken to see a man who was running a high fever. He was Captain "Grzybowski" (his real name was Skrzypek), and he had a huge abscess behind his left ear. While I examined him, I noticed that he was toying with a gun that had its safety catch released. I told him to put the gun away, as it would disturb me in my work, especially since I had decided to lance the abscess with no other anesthesia than a good swig of vodka. "Jim," who had brought me to "Grzybowski," explained my patient's behavior. "Grzybowski" was the district commander of all AL groups in the area. The NSZ had made several attempts on his life, and he did not trust anyone he did not know. Whatever suspicions he may have had about me were quickly put to rest, and I operated on him, with excellent results. The wound healed, and "Grzybowski" and I became the best of friends. (Several months later, the NSZ got "Grzybowski"; they killed him in an ambush.)

Several nights later a meeting took place at the cooperative store, and an official chain of command for the Southern District, Lublin Region, of the AL was set up. "Grab" (Jan) Wyderkowski (now a general in the Polish army) was named chief of staff; "Grzybowski," a farmer in civilian life, became chief of military, operations; "Jim" Czyzewski, chief of intelligence; and I, "Znachor," chief of the medical corps.

Since I was now the chief of the AL medical corps and also the only medical man in my unit, I set about at once to organize a medical corps. My first priority was to find badly needed medical and surgical supplies. Some of these items came to me as a gift from a sympathizer of our cause, Mr. Czerwinski, a pharmacist in Krasnik. Czerwinski also prevailed on other pharmacists to help us in this manner. At the same time, our boys raided unfriendly pharmacies and surgical supply houses to "confiscate" the materials we needed.

My next task was to create a medical staff. There simply were no doctors in our unit. We had notified headquarters in Warsaw of our need for medical personnel, but to no avail.

Within a very short time, I had assembled a group of women and organized a "school of nursing." The nurses got their practical training by accompanying me on my visits to patients. It was an "in-service" training course of sorts. I must say that these women learned quickly and became very proficient in their duties. My personal assistant — the best one on my staff — was "Jim"'s daughter, who was then all of thirteen years old. A very eager and intelligent girl, she hoped to become a registered nurse after the war. (I understand she attained her goal.) It was odd to see this teenager with an automatic gun on her shoulder and a bag of bandages in her hand. She used gun and bandages equally well whenever the need arose. Among the escaped Soviet POWs who had joined the AL I also found two medicos, whom I promptly coopted into my medical corps.

In addition to giving my students practical training, I periodically gave them informal lectures on hygiene, preventive medicine and, very important, taught them how to sterilize cloth for use as bandages. Sometimes, we used chemical methods of sterilization. But when necessary, we used a very primitive method: we pressed soaking wet material with hot irons until it was completely dry.

Most of the girls in our unit were local women who cared for the wounded soldiers in their area; others were regular partisans, fighting alongside the men.

Patients who were ambulatory spent their time in the woods. Bedridden patients were put up with families in the villages or in well-camouflaged hideouts. Each "foster family" was given instructions for evacuating the patient in case of danger. I must point out that, to my knowledge, no sick or wounded partisans were ever betrayed to the Germans, not even by those elements in the populace that had no use for partisans.

Eventually, we set up primitive "base hospitals" at various places in the woods. Medical rounds took a lot of time, the base hospitals grew larger, but no help was forthcoming from headquarters.

In time I acquired some medical instruments and splints. I could now perform minor surgery and do orthopedic work, mostly with fractures, simple and compound, caused by bullets. I took pride in the fact that, despite the primitive conditions under which I had to work, I lost very few patients. Much of the credit for this success was due to my staff, who were disciplined, efficient and at the same time compassionate.

At last, late in May, 1944, a doctor arrived. A native of Kielce or Kalisz (I do not remember which), he had been sent to us from Warsaw. His name was Jerzy Roth; his underground name was "Chentny" ("the Willing One"). He was to survive the war, but died of tuberculosis in 1945. By the time "Chentny" arrived, I had sufficient trained personnel, male and female, to attach a medical patrol to every partisan fighting group. However, my increased medical work did not keep me from participating also in military operations, mostly with the outfits of two of our most aggressive commanders, "Przepiorka" (The Quail") and "Cien" ("The Shadow") Kowalski.

I had developed very friendly relations with the civilian population of the area, to whom I never refused free medical help when they needed me. They all knew where and how to find me, whether in the village or in the woods. One night, while I was staying in a small settlement, I was called to Rzeczyca to deliver a baby. The mother, who happened to be the village midwife, had developed complications, and the midwife from the neighboring village, who had been called to help her, did not know what to do. I arrived just in time to extract a healthy, rather large boy. It was a breech presentation (buttocks first), as if the baby had been bent on showing the world exactly what he thought of it.

Since the establishment of the general staff for the district, the chiefs of the services met regularly to discuss the overall situation and to plan future operations against the

Germans and the enemies from within. I became very friendly with "Grab," "Jim," and with "Lis" ("The Fox"), an AL organizer whose real name was Tadeusz Szymanski.

We frequently discussed the problem of Jews and the partisan movement. Large Jewish groups were safe from internal enemies thanks to their size, their bravery, excellent commanders and their ample supplies of weapons, but smaller groups often fell prey to bands of NSZ or to ordinary bandits. On my recommendation an order went out to all field units to seek out these smaller units and incorporate them into the ranks of the AL. Their dependents were placed with peasant families, who found them places to hide.

One time, in February, 1944, "Grab" and I made plans to liberate Jews who had been interned in a labor camp in Krasnik. With the help of our contact man, a *Volksdeutscher,* we smuggled a few pistols and hand grenades into the camp. Our plans called for an attack on the guards from the inside and outside simultaneously. The operation was scheduled for the end of February, but unfortunately, the inmate leaders decided it was still too cold. Several days later, an argument between two of the inmates resulted in the exposure of the plot. The ringleaders were executed and many others were dispersed to other camps.

Six of the inmates managed to escape and join our AL unit. One of them asked to be called "Nili." This had been the name also of the Jewish underground intelligence group that had helped the British expel the Turks from Palestine during World War I. I never learned this man's real name or where he had come from. I saw him only twice: the first time when I welcomed him into our unit, and the second time when I found him dead in the final battle before our liberation. I am writing about him because he was an excellent radio technician. According to "Grab," who came to know him better, "Nili" had ambitious plans. He tried to construct a radio transmitter and make broadcasts to the entire free world, appealing for help in organizing a "Jewish Legion" like the one that had fought alongside the Allies in the Middle East during World War I, and informing the world outside about what was going on in the German labor and concentration camps. Unfortunately, the war progressed too rapidly, and "Nili" died before his dreams could be fulfilled.

Meanwhile, the battle lines drew steadily closer to our area. The Germans were continually "falling back to pre-selected positions" in order to shorten their front lines. They suffered heavy casualties. Transportation to and from the front became more and more difficult due to bombings from the air and constant acts of sabotage by the partisans on the ground.

At the same time, political activity increased inside Poland as well as in the Union of Polish Patriots, which was based in the Soviet Union. In May, 1944, a group of men who had been designated as the future leaders of the postwar provisional government of Poland were skillfully smuggled through the front lines into Russian-held territory by a partisan group under the leadership of Chil Grynszpan.

One day in June, our men derailed a train not far from Rzeczyca. There were some German casualties. A few civilian patients also suffered minor injuries. Several hours later, five well-dressed gentlemen, who looked like "cosmopolitan" types, entered the cooperative store. They told the manager, our agent "Kuma," that they had been on the way to Krasnik, but that their train had been sabotaged. Unwilling to wait for another train, they had decided to travel on foot to the nearest village, which happened to be Rzeczyca. After they had been given some refreshments, one of them, who seemed to be the top man in the group, asked whether he could speak to "Jim." Of course "Kuma" replied that she did not know anyone by that name. There must be some mistake, she said. At the same time, she made sure that somebody got hold of "Jim" or some other member of our general staff.

"Jim" was duly found and a careful interrogation of the five gentlemen revealed that they were the leaders of the provisional Polish government that had been named by the Union of Polish Patriots. They were General "Rola" Zymierski, minister of defense; "Kotek" Agroszewski, minister for internal affairs; Jan Czechowicz, minister of justice, and Dr. Litwin, minister of health. The fifth man was Litwin's son. It was our responsibility to give these dignitaries our care and protection and then, at the proper time, to smuggle them to the Russian side.

Meanwhile, the battle front continued moving toward our area, The Russians and the newly-formed Polish army kept up their steady pressure on the Germans. The Germans were harassed also from behind the lines. Military supplies intended for the *Wehrmacht* reached their destinations only after long delays or not at all, due to sabotage and ambushes. Communications were frequently disrupted.

All this—and I suspect they knew that the high command of the AL was in the area—caused the Germans to assign two divisions of infantry, artillery and air force to deal with the partisans. They surrounded several thousand partisans in the Lipskie and Janowski woods in a frantic attempt to eradicate the underground fighters and thus protect the retreating German forces.

In spite of these developments, General "Rola" Zymierski, together with the entire high command of the district, visited and inspected every available unit, giving instructions for future operations and, in general, conducting business as usual, except that we had to move our headquarters to Trzydnik because Rzeczyca had become a base for German operations.

The five-man delegation from Russia remained with us for about three weeks. During that period, they and we became good friends. I developed a special relationship with General "Rola" Zymierski. In addition to helping ensure his personal safety, I was also his physician. He believed in me and trusted me completely. This relationship was to continue until I left Poland, and we corresponded with one another even for some time after my departure.

During the first week of July, 1944, a Russian plane landed not far from the village of Szczecin, near Annopol, a place we considered suitable for a makeshift landing strip. General "Rola" Zymierski, along with Messrs. "Kotek" Agroszewski and Czechowicz, boarded the plane. Dr. Litwin and his son had left for Warsaw two weeks earlier. The plane's engine rumbled noisily and after a few minutes the machine was airborne. We were excited and applauded joyfully as the plane took off. But suddenly the plane tilted to one side and crashed from an altitude of about 100 feet.

We all ran toward the plane. General "Rola" Zymierski emerged first, followed by "Kotek" Agroszewski. They had escaped with relatively slight damage; the general sustained only superficial injuries, and "Kotek" Agroszewski had a fracture of the right wrist. Mr. Czechowicz was not so fortunate. He had to be removed from the plane with a compound fracture of the kneecap and simple fractures of both bones in the right leg.

The pilot said that the plane was a total loss. He dismounted a machine gun from the cockpit and then set fire to the plane.

The night was almost gone. Soon daylight would come. We knew we had to escape in a hurry; the Germans would almost certainly discover the burned-out shell of the plane and investigate further. "Jim" and I transported Mr. Czechowicz to a safe place, passing by a garrison of Polish police, who fortunately paid us no attention. I attended to Mr. Czechowicz's injuries as well as I could, and gave him some medication to deaden his pain. Then I left him to help the other victims of the ill-fated takeoff and to confer with other members of the general staff about further action.

Our most difficult problem was how to notify the Union of Polish Patriots about the loss of the plane. For that purpose we would need a radio transmitter. By now there were in our area many well-equipped Russian partisan groups; some of these had radio transmitters. But most of them were engaged in battle in the woods. We had to obtain access to a transmitter as soon as possible, because our situation had been compromised by the accident. Once again, I found that my knowledge of Russian came in handy.

That same night, I moved toward the Lipskie woods at the head of four volunteers in search of a radio transmitter. In one area we had to pass a railroad crossing. At that time attacks and sabotage raids on trains were almost daily occurrences. The Germans had stationed sentries at every crossing and we could easily be ambushed. As we negotiated the crossing, I devised a plan to prevent our being caught. We "mobilized" five horse-drawn wagons with drivers from the area. I instructed the drivers to be boisterous, make a big show of smoking cigarettes, and to stop at the crossing. My plan was based on the assumption that if there were German guards on the other side of the crossing, they would probably let the first wagon, the "reconnaissance vehicle," pass, and wait to ambush the wagons that followed, which they would expect to carry the main body of the raiders.

I chose one of the five wagons to lead the crossing to the other side. The four other wagons took their places behind it as if to follow the lead wagon. I myself took over as driver of the "reconnaissance vehicle." This was in fact the wagon that carried our entire group; the four volunteers were lying on the bottom of the wagon, under a blanket of hay. The other four wagons, driven by local men, had no passengers. I drove along slowly, calmly puffing at a cigarette and talking to the horses.

My wagon passed over the crossing unhindered and kept on going. About ten minutes later, as we had agreed, the other four wagons turned around and sped toward home. They were pursued by a burst of machine gun fire from the German guards, but the drivers and horses were not hit.

Meanwhile, the wagon that I was driving and that contained our men continued safely on its mission and, two days later, we returned to our base with a radio transmitter. Ironically, however, our expedition proved to have been unnecessary. For the day after our departure from Trzydnik, a Russian communications crew assigned permanently to our area had arrived at our base and had notified the Union of Polish Patriots in Kiev of the plane crash.

The Union of Polish Patriots promised to send another plane for the general and the two other delegates but gave us no definite date on which to expect the plane. Mean-

111

while, Mr. Czechowicz began to run a temperature and I could do nothing for him except change his bandages. Since he was a very important personage — Poland's future minister of justice — I did not want to assume the responsibility for his care myself. I therefore decided to arrange for a consultation with a surgeon from the nearest city, Lublin.

I called for Elvira, one of my partisan nurse-couriers, a very brave, intelligent young woman, I instructed her to take a wagon to Lublin, locate a surgeon and bring him to our base. I detailed two boys to travel with her. We agreed that she would return the next morning.

That evening, however, we received a message that a small plane had been dispatched to pick up the general and Messrs. Agroszewski and Czechowicz, from our base and take them to Kiev. But by that time Elvira had left and there was no way for us to inform her that no surgeon would be needed now.

We all went to the landing strip to meet the plane, which landed on schedule on our landing strip near Goscieradow. General "Rola" Zymierski and "Kotek" Agroszewski climbed into the plane under their own power. Mr. Czechowicz and three seriously wounded partisans had to be carried aboard the plane. We wished them luck. This time the plane took off safely. On our way back to the base we heard anti-aircraft artillery and saw searchlights scan the skies, but several hours later we picked up a message that the plane with its important passengers aboard had landed safely in Kiev.

Meanwhile, Elvira and her two escorts, dressed in peasant attire, had arrived in Lublin. Not having any contacts and not knowing any doctors in the city, they roamed the streets of Lublin looking for a shingle with the words

"Physician-Surgeon" on it. Eventually, they managed to locate a surgeon. But how were they to persuade him to come with them?

Elvira devised a plan. She knocked wildly at the door of the surgeon's office and put on a convincing act of hysteria. Her child, she cried, had been in an accident and was lying in the street, badly hurt. The doctor immediately put on his coat and followed the distraught young woman to the wagon that was waiting outside.

To his surprise, instead of the bleeding, broken body of a child, the doctor was met by two healthy men pointing their machine guns at him. He was warned not to make any noise. He was also told that nothing would happen to him. He would merely be taken to see a patient.

When the doctor arrived at our base, he was deathly pale and shaking like a leaf. I introduced myself to him as a colleague, Dr. Znachor. He said he had heard of me. I explained why we had sent for him, namely, to treat a badly wounded man, a partisan. Unfortunately, this patient was no longer with us. He had been evacuated by plane to Kiev on sudden notice.

Gradually, the good doctor regained his composure. We were all hungry, so we sat down to eat. The food was good; there was plenty of meat, which slid down easily with liberal amounts of vodka. Before long, the doctor relaxed and started to talk about himself. His name, he said, was Oziemba. He had come to Lublin from the Poznan area and he hated the Germans. His tongue loosened by the vodka, he said what he would like to do to the Germans, expressing his feelings in language that made even the partisans blush, especially since a number of women were also present. We allowed him to rest for a few hours, then explained to him that Elvira and her two escorts would take him back to Lublin. Before he left we made him swear not to tell anyone where he had been or to talk about anything he had seen or heard at our base—not even to his wife. And so the doctor, accompanied by Elvira and her two helpers, left on his merry way home.

* * *

The fighting in the Lublin area ceased in July, 1944. I still remained in Krasnik for a while to liquidate my "base hospitals" and place my patients into real hospitals, under good medical care. Early in September, I came to Lublin. I had a Gentile friend there, Dr. Stephen Witkowski, who had been a classmate of mine. I found him working in the local hospital. We were both happy to see each other again. After we had exchanged memories of the war years, I asked him whether he had ever heard of a Dr. Oziemba. He said he knew him very well, and that he was a good man. However, something had happened to him several months ago. He had always been calm and pleasant but gradually he had become irritable, tense and secretive. There were also rumors that his marriage was in trouble. The change in him had begun after he had suddenly disappeared from town for two days, Dr. Witkowski told me.

I wanted to see Dr. Oziemba. Dr. Witkowski took me to his place. I was still wearing my partisan outfit. I had a huge revolver in my holster, a machine gun over my shoulders and an ammunition belt over my chest, with two hand grenades attached to it.

Dr. Witkowski knocked on the door and asked whether Dr. Oziemba could see him and a friend. We entered the room. I immediately felt sorry for having surprised the unfortunate man. Oziemba, a man with a healthy complexion, became pale as a sheet and almost fainted when he

114

saw me in full fighting gear. His first words were, "I didn't tell anybody anything! I don't know anything! I've never seen you before! I've never even heard of you!"

Dr. Witkowski observed the scene in bewilderment. It took me some time and a considerable amount of explaining until Dr. Oziemba regained his calm and Dr. Witkowski understood what had happened.

"Can I talk about it now—I mean, where I was that time?" Dr. Oziemba diffidently inquired. "Or is it still a secret?"

"No," I replied, "It's not a secret anymore."

Dr. Oziemba brightened visibly. "That's good," he said. "Now I can straighten things out with my wife."

We parted as good friends. I never saw Dr. Oziemba again, but Dr. Witkowski kept me informed about him and his wife. It seemed that after our meeting in Lublin, Dr. Oziemba had become his old self again, and Dr. and Mrs. Oziemba were once again the loving couple they had been before the "consultation" at the partisan base.

CHAPTER SEVEN

Two
Journeys

In the middle of July, 1944, I started out on one of my medical rounds. The war in our area was drawing to a close. The German army was retreating on the Russian front. The headquarters of our area had moved from Rzeczyca into the woods near the village of Budki. We felt quite safe there, because we knew that the Germans were afraid of the woods, the more so since they did not know how many partisans they would encounter there. The main objective of the German troops was to reach and cross the bridge near Annopol. Hunting for partisans would only delay their orderly retreat.

I had finished my rounds in the village of Grabowka and vicinity, where I had spent two or three days. An elderly peasant came for me in his wagon to take me back to the partisan base. The wagon was drawn by two horses; its seat was a bale of hay covered with a blanket. I put my machine gun beside me and covered it with hay. I hid my two handguns under my raincoat.

After we had traveled for about thirty minutes, we reached the paved highway. My driver stopped abruptly. As far as one could see, the highway was jammed with retreating Germans. In addition to long columns of infantry, there were columns of motorized units, following one another at intervals of about 100 feet. My driver got off the wagon and walked over to the highway to see whether there was room for us. He returned with the news that the motorized units were being followed by another column of tanks and artillery perhaps a mile long. We might have to wait for hours before we would be able to get onto the highway. In addition, he felt that we should lie low because there were German soldiers resting on either side of the highway, wherever they could find some shade.

I decided that we should wait for the cavalcade of defeat to pass. But after about half an hour, I changed my mind. I realized that it would be much more difficult to travel on the highway at night. The Germans would be even more watchful at night and would surely stop anyone who would try to get onto the highway then.

I instructed my driver to move onto the highway as soon as there was a gap in the marching units. "But they'll kill us!" he lamented. When my arguments did not help, I told him that if he did not do as I said I would kill him myself. This gentle persuasion worked. He leaped back onto the driving seat and we fairly galloped into the first gap that opened up in the seemingly endless columns of tanks and artillery. I urged him not to go fast. Even through the noise of the marching soldiers, the thunder of the tanks and the squeaks of our own wagon wheels, I could hear him murmuring prayers. I did not blame him; his life was in dire peril—and so was mine.

Here was a long column of German military vehicles proceeding in an orderly procession, and in its midst one horse-drawn wagon with only one passenger—a partisan fighter, armed to the teeth, the worst kind of enemy the Germans knew. Even worse, I was a Jew. I did not care to think what would happen if the Germans caught me.

However, there was no way out of the predicament in which I now found myself. It was too late for the wagon to turn back. All that my driver and I could do was watch for the next dirt road, get off the highway, and so remove us from the German columns.

From time to time, weary German soldiers jumped on our wagon to rest their battered feet. Some of them attempted to engage me in conversation. I pretended to be a *Volksdeutscher* and exchanged cigarettes with them. Usually, the poor fellows would curse the war and express the hope that it would end soon, so that they would be able to return to their homes and families. Of course, I heartily agreed with them, watching all the time for a chance to turn off the highway.

I began to question the wisdom of the order I had given my driver. We should never had gotten onto this accursed highway to begin with. But the damage had been done. I became philosophical about the situation into which I had put myself. I had been in many tight spots before, but I never had to deal with an entire motorized German army before. Ever since the war began, I had made myself confront the possibility that I might be killed. What had changed over the years was my attitude toward death. Gradually, my fear of dying had changed to indifference, then to resignation, and finally to anger. If I had to die, I was determined to die fighting and would take some Germans with me. I was no longer a hunted animal; I had become a hunter myself. As I sat in the wagon on the highway, surrounded by Hitler's forces in full retreat, I marveled at this change in me. My thoughts strayed back to another journey, one that I had made two years earlier, from the Warsaw ghetto to the town of Hrubieszow. I knew that this was not the time to recall the past, but I could not help remembering...

* * *

After the mass deportation of June 8, 1942, the Jewish community of Grabowiec had ceased to exist. When I returned to Grabowiec after jumping from the deportation train, I found that of 2,000 Jews only about 300 had returned from the Mionchin railroad station. Hardly a complete family was left—most of the Jews left in Grabowiec were wives without husbands, husbands without wives, and children without parents. The others had been "resettled"—as I found out later—in the death camp of Sobibor. The old, the sick, the crippled and the little children had been shot as soon as the train had pulled out of the station, and had been piled into a mass grave in the station yard.

After the deportation, the gendarmes moved out of Grabowiec. The Jews who had remained there accommodated themselves as well as they could, and life went on.

But I felt I could not stay in Grabowiec any longer. During the one year I had lived and worked there, the place had become home to me. The Jews of Grabowiec had become my brothers and sisters; the children, the sons and daughters I had never had. Now, in one single day, I had lost my family all over again. True, I had many Gentile friends, close and faithful friends, but that was not the same.

In the middle of July, about a month after my return to Grabowiec, I decided to go back to Warsaw, where I had studied and where I had lived late in 1940 and again during the first half of 1941. I knew that there were now about half a million Jews locked up in the Warsaw ghetto. Surely, I thought, I should be able to find my place among them. I felt that I would be safer there than in the countryside. The Germans would never dare to wipe out a ghetto of half a million people. The world would not stand for it.

122

I obtained false travel documents stating that I was permitted to travel between Hrubieszow and Warsaw in order to purchase medical supplies for labor camps and German farms around Hrubieszow, which, as I have already mentioned, was not far from Grabowiec. Armed with these documents, I boarded a train bound for Warsaw.

In Warsaw, I made my way into the ghetto. The outside world, with its fresh air, its flowers, its trees and its human dignity, closed behind me.

I adjusted quickly to the ghetto. Some of my friends were still there. I even found a job—as a night doctor at the Toebbens plant on Prosta Street. This was a German factory working for the Wehrmacht *and employing Jews from the ghetto.*

Then, on July 22, 1942, disaster caught up with the Warsaw ghetto. Deportations began. Life became more difficult by the day. The Judenrat *constantly received new quotas of Jews to round up for "resettlement." The German noose around the ghetto tightened.*

Early in August, the "Little Ghetto" was evacuated and the population ordered to move into the "Big Ghetto" within two or three days. Any Jew caught in the "Little Ghetto" after that deadline was gunned down on the spot. The Judenrat *headquarters moved from Grzybowska Street to a new location on Ogrodowa Street. Some of the Jews from the Toebbens plant were taken away with the others. I was among the Jews left in place but I did not want to remain there and decided to transfer myself to the branch of Toebbens that was located in the building of what had once been the Konarski High School on Leszno Street.*

Walking through the streets of the "Little Ghetto" was a nightmare. The neighborhood that always had been so noisy before was now as quiet as a churchyard. The streets, once so crowded, were empty now except for dead bodies that lay on the ground unburied—on the sidewalks, in courtyards and in the gutters. I entered the house on Ciepla 6, where I had once stayed with a family named Gothelf. No one was there now. The Gothelf apartment was a shambles. As I left the house, I ran into Mrs. Sztoltzman, who had also stayed with the Gothelfs. She told me that she had gone into hiding during the great "resettlement operation" of July 22. I asked her to come with me, but she refused. She told me that she must wait for her family to come back.

It was on the small square on Ciepla and Krochmalna Streets that I ran into Ele Baumsecer, who had been king of Warsaw's Jewish underworld before the war. Now he had become a hero because he managed to smuggle food into the ghetto. He, too, refused to join me in my quest for safety. He told me that his family and his fiancée had been taken to the Umschlagplatz, the assembly point for deportation, and that he was on his way to join them there and give himself up.

I made my way across the wooden bridge that spanned Chlodna Street and finally reached Leszno Street. I met one of my former teachers, a well-known pediatrician, Dr. Bussel, and his family. We were joined by another physician, Dr. Grynberg, better known among his friends as "Redhead." We were to organize medical services at the Toebbens plant.

The next morning, I went to the new Judenrat headquarters on Ogrodowa Street. I hoped to find out what the foreseeable future might hold in store for us. No one seemed to know for sure, but rumors and conjectures were rife. There was talk of putting up a fight, of organizing armed

124

resistance in the ghetto. A commotion started. I quietly left the building and headed for the comparative safety of the Toebbens plant.

The following morning I was called to treat an injured person on the first floor of the plant in the Konarski High School building. Just as I finished bandaging the patient, Dr. Bussel's six-year old son came looking for me. "Father said you should not come down just now," the little boy told me. "You have a visitor." I understood at once that I was in serious trouble, for otherwise Dr. Bussel would not have exposed his child to danger by sending him to look for me. I remembered the talk about armed resistance at Judenrat *headquarters the day before. The Gestapo must be after me. I jumped from the window into the yard below. The ground of the school building extended to Nowolipki Street. I reached this street and proceeded to No.14, where I had been staying with a family named Silberman. I found the place deserted. A member of the ghetto police told me that all the Jews in the block, including the Silbermans, had already been taken to the* Umschlagplatz *for deportation. The ghetto was no longer a safe place.*

I stopped at the Silberman apartment only long enough to pick up my small suitcase in which I had one pair of underwear, one bottle each of pure alcohol and cologne, and my permit to travel between Hrubieszow and Warsaw. Then I left the house and headed for the ghetto gate on Nowolipki Street.

The gate was open but guarded by two members of the ghetto police, one Polish policeman and one German gendarme. I noticed the German first, for just as I stepped through the gate into the "Aryan Sector" of the city, I heard a shot behind me. I turned around just in time to see the

125

German returning his gun to its holster. A bearded Jew, blood running from his head, lay on the ground motionless. I hesitated. Perhaps I should walk back into the ghetto. But it was too late. The gendarme had already noticed me.

"Come here!" he shouted. He took me into a wooden shack that apparently served as an office for the guards at the ghetto gate. "You're a Jew," he said. He was not asking me a question; he was making a statement. He looked at the Star of David on my arm, then pointed to the dead man on the ground. "You see what happened to that Jew. He tried to cross over to the Aryan sector. What are you doing here?" He appeared to be calm, talking to me as if he had not killed a man only minutes ago. His voice actually sounded friendly.

I showed him my papers. "Oh, so you're from out of town!" he exclaimed. "You're not a resident of the Warsaw ghetto? Going back to your patients out in the sticks, are you? Don't you know it's dangerous for a Jew to travel?"

"I know," I replied. "But I'm needed at the German plant and on the German farms, where Jews are working."

The gendarme actually seemed to understand. "You look tired and hungry," he said and handed me a ham sandwich. Then he opened my suitcase and saw the bottle of alcohol inside. He warned me that this alcohol might be regarded as contraband and I might get into trouble. I offered to give him the alcohol and the cologne, but he refused the gift. "A good German doesn't take other people's possessions," he said.

To this day I do not understand what I had done to rate such courteous treatment from a German gendarme. Perhaps he had already filled his quota of Jewish arrests and liquidations for the day and could afford to be friendly. He kept going in and out of the shack. Behind me, I could

126

*hear the sound of whips against human flesh and shouted
orders, "Back inside the ghetto, you Jew swine!" But I did
not hear any more shooting.*

*I do not know how long I remained at the ghetto gate. It
was getting dark. Finally, the gendarme returned to me.
"Look," he said, "I have a wagon and driver waiting. He
has instructions from me. He'll take you to the railroad
station. It's dark already, so nobody will notice you and
ask questions. Go! Oh—and—good luck!"*

*I was flabbergasted and more than a little suspicious,
but here I was, alive and unharmed, in a horse-drawn wagon with a driver apparently ready to take me wherever I
wanted to go. I was out of the ghetto!*

*In the "Aryan sector," I decided to stop off for a brief
visit with a good friend, one of the smugglers who, together with his wife, frequently commuted between Warsaw
and Grabowiec. I knew the address: it was Prozna 8. I had
been a frequent visitor in that building during my student
days. At that time a classmate of mine, Dr. Alexander
Izgur, had lived there, and a prominent attorney by the
name of Zundelewicz.*

*I asked the driver to drop me off on Grzybowski Square.
The driver did not want to be paid. He did not want to see
where I was going, and drove off in a hurry. I looked
around. The street was empty. I made my way to Prozna 8
and climbed up to the third floor. My friend's wife opened
the door and almost fainted when she saw me. She knew
that I had left Grabowiec for Warsaw, but she had not expected to see me alive. She started to fix something for me
to eat but, as she told me later, I fell asleep on the sofa and
did not wake up until the next morning.*

*The one train that left Warsaw to Hrubieszow each day
left at seven o'clock in the morning. So, as soon as I awoke,*

127

my hostess and a friend of hers who lived in the same building took me to the Main Railroad Terminal. They bought me a railroad ticket to Hrubieszow, wished me good luck and left.

At first, everything went smoothly, but not for long. My troubles began when I attempted to board the train. The platform was packed with people, mostly smugglers. There was pushing and shoving; people were screaming and cursing each other. The compartment in which I wanted to sit was already filled and I, who until then had tried to be as inconspicuous as possible, became more aggressive. A young train guard, a Volksdeutscher, *noticed me and dragged me off the steps of the car. "This is the end of my trip, and also for me," I said to myself.*

The man examined my papers. They had expired and he probably suspected that they had been forged. "Let's go to the police station," he said. "It's not far from here. Anyway, as far as you're concerned, this is the end of the line." The police station was on the second floor of a building on Poznanska Street. Halfway up the staircase we stopped.

"How much cash do you have on you?" the train guard wanted to know.

I opened my wallet and pulled out 1,000 zlotys.

"Is that all?" he asked.

"Sorry, but that's all I have," I replied.

He counted out 1,000 zlotys and put them into his pocket. "Let's go back to the railroad station," he said. "I don't want your blood on my hands."

I did not know whether to be happy or sad. If I had already endured so much at the beginning of my journey out of Warsaw, what would be in store for me later?

At the station, the guard left me and I was alone. But of course the train had left, and the next train would leave only at seven o'clock the next morning. What was I to do in the meantime? I was hungry, thirsty, hot, tired and scared. Would this macabre drama ever end?

Suddenly, I remembered a young Pole whom I had befriended at Stalag IA: Colonel Korzeniowski, the son of a prominent eye specialist. We had become very close and shared everything. Because I was much older than he and already a doctor, he looked up to me as a father figure. One day he showed me a gold cross on a thin gold chain. He said that his grandmother had given it to him on the day he was drafted into the Polish army. He confided to me that he would sell it to the company clerk, a Volksdeutscher, for some cigarettes and bread. I told him that he must not do such a thing. I got him ten cigarettes free of charge from a doctor in the infirmary and gave him my own daily ration of bread in exchange for his solemn promise that he would never sell his grandmother's gift. I remembered that Korzeniowski had written home about me, and I also recalled the old lady's name and address. She lived on Krucza Street, not far from the railroad station. I decided to look her up.

A very distinguished-looking, gray-haired lady opened the door. She looked me up and down. Her eyes came to rest on the Star of David on my arm. I do not know what her grandson had told her about me in his letters, but her first words to me were, "You are Dr. Temchin."

She opened the door wide and, spent as I was, I almost fell into the room. She assisted me to a chair and prepared breakfast for both of us. During the meal she mentioned that my young friend had been released from the prison camp, that he was living in Warsaw and that, in fact, she was expecting him to visit her that evening.

I slept almost all that day at the old lady's apartment. At about seven o'clock in the evening Korzeniowski arrived. Yes, he said, he still had the cross and chain. When it got darker, he took me to the station, walking at some distance ahead of me in case I was stopped. Finally he waved a silent good-by to me and disappeared into the crowd. I found myself in the hall of the station, trying to become quite invisible.

The station was less crowded than it had been in the morning. There were only a few civilians but many German soldiers. I saw one group of soldiers huddled together in a corner. I overheard them agreeing to spend the night there in the station, waiting for the morning train. Rank-and-file Wehrmacht *men, especially when they were off duty, were not particularly interested in bothering with Jews. So I decided to sit down near them, with my Star of David partly hidden by my overcoat. If I sat there, I reasoned, it would look as if I were somehow connected with these soldiers and no one would stop to ask me embarrassing questions.*

The night passed uneventfully. I even managed to sleep a little. At about 6:30 the next morning I started moving with the crowd toward the platform, battling my way toward the train for Hrubieszow. As on the day before, all the compartments were already filled. I despaired of ever being able to get aboard this train. Then I noticed the train guard I had encountered the morning before. He saw me, too, but he did not seem to remember me. In fact, he pushed me into the compartment. The doors of the car were closed; the train moved back, then lurched forward, and I was on my way back to Grabowiec.

After a few minutes, the passengers had settled down

130

for the long ride. Those who had boarded first had found seats; others were still standing, holding on to the walls or to one another. Most of the passengers were smugglers, carrying dry goods, tools and other articles they had bought in Warsaw and that were not available in the countryside. They would exchange these things for food and produce to sell in the city. They started to discuss how best to hide their goods from the gendarmes who were walking up and down the aisles of the cars.

Then they noticed me, and the Star of David showing partly from under my coat. "Zhyd!" ("Jew!") someone whispered. All talk ceased abruptly and everyone in the car seemed to be looking in my direction. The passengers were exchanging meaningful glances. "What do you think of that? There's a Jew in this car!"

After a while, some of the passengers began to ask me questions. Who was I? Didn't I know that my presence on the train endangered the lives of everyone else in the car— quite aside of all the merchandise they would lose if I attracted the attention of the gendarmes? I knew they were right, but I wanted to live also.

Someone suggested that I should be thrown off the train; others were for handing me over to the authorities at the next stop. But there were others who took my side. I had the same right to live as anybody else, they said. Besides, it would be un-Christian to turn me over to the Germans. We were Poles, they said. We still have some honor left. I did not participate in the argument, for I knew whatever I might say would only make things worse for me. I was a passive observer, completely helpless, resigned to my fate.

Gradually my intercessors got the upper hand. One young man went so far as to suggest that my presence might be a blessing in disguise. The smugglers decided they would try

131

to protect me by moving me from place to place and by crowding around me to hide me from view in case the car was searched. If I was caught, they would pretend that they had not noticed my Star of David. In return for their indulgence, I would then tell the gendarmes that all the contraband was mine.

The atmosphere brightened. I was offered food, even some vodka. The passengers became friendly and talkative. They exchanged the latest news and gossip and questioned me about life in the ghetto.

After about one hour, the train came to a stop. Two gendarmes entered our compartment. They looked at the bundles the passengers had placed on their seats and on the floor. They threw a few of them out the window, without even examining their contents. They also checked a few identity papers. Whenever the gendarmes seemed to be turning or looking in my direction, my fellow passengers managed to screen me from their view. Everyone heaved a sigh of relief when the two Germans finally got off. At least one hurdle had been overcome, and we were safe until the next stop.

The train moved on. At the next station some passengers left our car and new people got on. The original passengers still did their best to protect me. They did not tell the newcomers about the "human contraband" in the car until the train was in motion again.

At nearly every stop, gendarmes or train guards boarded the train to make an inspection. Judging from their behavior, the guards seemed to know most of the passengers from previous encounters. The searches were not too thorough because most of the inspectors had been bribed in advance with gifts or cash.

I tried not to attract attention to myself. I spoke to no one but spent most of the time in a corner under one of the seats. The monotonous rhythm of the train made me sleepy and unable to think. This was a blessing, for in my lucid moments I saw Ciepla Stret in Warsaw with all the unburied corpses, and the scene at Mionchin station, where I had saved Baby S. Why had I saved her? What further cruelties did life hold in store for her?

At one station the train made a longer stop. Gendarmes were approaching our compartment and we heard a sharp whistle. Something was happening in the compartment nearest the locomotive. All the guards had been summoned to that spot. Apparently, it was something serious. The entire compartment was evacuated; one man had been taken off the train and led into the station building. I did not see any of this myself, but my fellow passengers gave me minute-by-minute descriptions of the scene. The man had been beaten up; blood was running from his mouth. When he did not walk fast enough to suit them, the gendarmes dragged him on. Finally a shot rang out. Then all was quiet and the train slowly pulled out of the station.

Who was that man? Why had he been taken off the train and beaten up? "Oh, he probably wasn't anyone special," was the consensus in the car. "Maybe a Jew." One of the passengers suggested that this incident, too, had been a godsend. It had probably saved our compartment from inspection. I wondered whether, at one of the next stops, I, too, would be caught and thus save my fellow passengers from the embarrassment of being caught as smugglers. In that case, I noted wrily, I would not have died in vain—at least as far as those smugglers were concerned.

133

What a thought! I never did learn the identity of the unfortunate man who had been taken off the train and probably killed. He might have been a Jew, or a Polish anti-Nazi.

As the train neared its destination, my compartment emptied noticeably. The inspections became very superficial. One gendarme asked me where I was going but he did not ask to see my papers and apparently did not notice my Star of David, still partially concealed by my overcoat. At last we reached familiar territory. I toyed with the idea of getting off at Mionchin Station and walking the rest of the way to Grabowiec. But that would be ten miles and I was too tired for that. I decided to stay on until Hrubieszow and rest with some friends there before proceeding to Grabowiec.

In the station I found a driver who took me into town. He let me off in the center of town and did not accept my fare. He wished me good luck and vanished down the street.

Several minues later I knocked at the door of a friend of mine, Dr. Fryderyk Orenstein, who lived in Hrubieszow with his mother and sister. They let me in, helped me to the couch, and gave me something to drink. They then began to ask me all kinds of questions but I did not answer because I had fallen asleep.

* * *

All this had happened two years earlier. Now, once again, I found myself traveling in the midst of my enemies. How would I ever get back to the partisan base?

After the wagon had crept along the highway for about half an hour, I noticed a narrow dirt road on our left. "Here's where we turn off, I'm afraid," I said to the Ger-

134

man soldiers who were on the wagon. Then I told my driver to turn off the highway. With more enthusiasm than necessary, he drove the horses off the highway with such speed that the wagon almost turned over. That would have been all we needed. My driver was praying aloud, but when we reached the dirt road his prayers ended with some juicy obscenities addressed to the Germans.

It was dark when we finally arrived at the partisan base. We were stopped by a sentry from one of our units. After I had said the proper password, my driver and I joined the rest of the partisans. After a good meal and a hearty swig of vodka, the driver told the willing listeners the story of how we had "made it," even though the Germans had known that we were partisans. The Germans, he asserted, had actually been afraid of us!

At the base I was briefed on important developments that had taken place during my absence. The Germans were retreating rapidly. According to the intelligence gathered by our unit, the retreat was hampered by frequent bombings from the Soviet air force. I was elated and proud of myself for having made some contribution to the war effort and to the final victory that now seemed at hand. I recalled the last two years, my journey from Warsaw to Hrubieszow and the journey I had just made, surrounded by people who would not have minded to see me die.

Now the Germans were about to go down in defeat. A brave new world would arise — along with a new Poland. A new Provisional Government was already established in Lublin, with a Jewish member, Dr. Emil Sommerstein, my future father-in-law, as a part of it. The date was July 22, 1944.

CHAPTER EIGHT

Captured by the Russians

The German army was in headlong retreat on the entire Russian-German front, trying to reach and cross the Vistula over the only bridge in this region, the bridge at Annopol. As I have already mentioned, our unit, ever since the departure of the delegation of the future Polish government leaders for Kiev, had a Russian communications unit attached to it. This unit reported on the numbers and movements of German troops with great accuracy on the basis of data supplied by our excellent intelligence service. Whenever a large unit, especially a motorized one, appeared near the Annopol bridge, Soviet planes immediately appeared, dropping their bombs and inflicting heavy casualties on the enemy.

The situation at the front was good, but we, the partisans, found ourselves in a vise between the advancing Soviet and Polish armies and the retreating Germans. The Russian strategy was to permit masses of German vehicles and men to accumulate at the approaches to bridges such as the one at Annopol, and then bomb them all at one time. Therefore, the Russians were not interested in destroying the Annopol bridge. They needed it as a bait for the Germans.

In their eagerness to make a fast retreat, the German forces moved westward along a very wide front, taking over almost every village on their way. That was why our general staff had to leave Rzeczyca. We went west into the areas of Goscieradow, Krasnik and Annopol, where there were many smaller wooded areas in addition to the main forest of Goscieradow.

Large numbers of civilians, young and old, now joined us in the woods. Whole families came with us, sometimes in wagons piled high with their household possessions.

The Germans utilized every negotiable path and dirt road for the westward movement of their troops. The sounds of battle were coming closer all the time. At first it seemed like thunder in the distance, but this was no thunder. It was bombs and artillery shells.

Because of the unpredictable movements of the Germans, our general staff split up into small groups in order to stay out of the enemy's sight. We had with us in the woods about eighty men. We had received, and passed on, orders not to attack the retreating Germans, but some hot-headed lower-echelon commander, seeing only small units of Germans, decided to act on his own. A fierce battle ensued, because it turned out that these small units were only spearheads of a larger contingent of motorized and infantry detachments. Although we inflicted heavy casualties upon the enemy, we lost many of our own men in this unnecessary battle.

On the other hand, along with a regimental flag and many German medals, we captured plans for the German retreat, and we also took one interesting prisoner. He was a noncommissioned officer, a mechanical engineer by profession. He claimed he was an anti-Nazi and had been forced to join the *Wehrmacht* against his convictions. He agreed to join us and even told us where we could expect the next contingent of Germans to turn up. Somehow, this man inspired confidence. We gave him back his rifle and told him to call on his compatriots to lay down their arms. Unfortunately, on his very first encounter with the Ger-

140

mans as a member of our partisan unit—on July 27 and 28, 1944—he was killed by a German officer.

At one point, several comrades and I, among them two women—one of the girls was "Polka" (her real name was Waclawa Marek)—somehow became separated from the others. There was no sign of the enemy and we must have let down our guard when suddenly, seemingly from out of nowhere, we were attacked by a group of Germans. This encounter did not last long. We wiped out the German patrol, but we lost three of our men and "Polka," who had joined our ranks only a few months earlier as a parachutist from the Soviet Union.

Tired and grieving for our dead comrades, we went out in search of our unit. I remembered an abandoned barn not far from the village of Budki. I suggested that we find it and stop there to orient ourselves. After about a quarter of an hour of wandering between a coppice and a thick forest, I saw the barn. Several others were already there, including Wicek, our chief of military operations, along with "Grab" and "Jim." We told them of our losses, then talked over what we would do next.

We were sure that the retreating Germans would soon turn off the main highway and make for the woods. "Jim" and I went to reconnoiter a ravine not far away, where we thought we could spend the night. We were about 300 feet away when we sighted Germans at the edge of the woods. In order to slow them down, Wicek engaged them in a fight and, utilizing a heavy growth of tall weeds for cover, he kept moving backward in the direction of the ravine where "Jim" and I were headed. "Jim" and I realized that the Germans were planning an encircling maneuver to trap Wicek's group. The fight proved costly to us, but even more so to the Germans,

141

We noticed, on our right flank, one German patrol of about ten men moving forward rapidly, not participating in the skirmish. Wicek was not aware of this, but their aim was to close the route of escape for our men. We had to thwart that strategy.

Without uttering a word, as if in response to an unspoken command, "Jim" and I opened fire on the Germans on the right flank. They were taken by surprise; they did not even have time to shoot back. I do not know how many of them escaped alive. "Jim" and I ran to join our comrades. On my way, I picked up a light machine gun from one of our comrades who lay on the ground, dead. It was "Nili," who had dreamed of underground radio broadcasts and the creation of a new Jewish Legion.

"Chentny," our first doctor, was also among the missing. But later I learned that he had made contact with another partisan unit that eventually crossed the battle front and found itself on Russian-held territory.

Our unit, very much diminished, reached the ravine. The nurses and I had our hands full, treating the wounded. Night came. Our soldiers were dead tired. We, the leaders, took over guard duty and let them get some sleep. We all would need our strength for the coming day.

The night passed in relative calm. Occasional bursts of machine-gun fire, the roar of airplanes overhead, the explosions of bombs and artillery did not disturb us. We had become accustomed to these noises of battle.

Ironically, during my years in prison camp, in the ghettos and in the partisan movement, I had not been particularly disturbed about the possibility of my getting killed. I had resigned myself to living one day at a time. I felt that I had no control over my own life. It was always others— German guards, SS men, the Polish "Blue Police"—who determined whether I would live or die, and what I would do. But now, on the threshold of freedom, I was sad to think that I might be killed at any moment and that all the hardships I had endured would then have been in vain. It would be tragic if I died without being able to see the new world that would emerge from the ruins of the war. This depressed me. I felt guilty for harboring such thoughts but I was only human and, now that the war was about to end, the prospects of a normal life at long last were too bright for me to ignore.

I must have fallen asleep for a while. When I awoke it was already broad daylight. The ravine was crowded with partisans and with people from nearby farms, along with their children and their livestock. Everyone was quiet. All necessary conversation was conducted in whispers. Even the little children and the animals were quiet. "Grab" ordered the partisans to conceal their weapons as best as they could. This was a precautionary measure.

From time to time, German soldiers passed close to us. If they were to see us with our weapons, they might engage us in battle in territory and under conditions that were definitely not favorable to us. Quite aside from the threat to our own lives, we had to consider the danger to the innocent villagers who had taken shelter with us in the ravine.

The day dawned hot but bright. Despite the silence around us, we could feel a heaviness in the air. We heard the monotonous tramp of the boots of marching soldiers and, from time to time, the whistle and boom of bombs from the direction of the Annopol bridge.

I crawled to the top of the ravine several times, hoping to make my way into the village of Upper Budki to find out the latest news. But each time I had to retreat, because it was clear that no one would be able to reach the village. Germans were everywhere, as far as the eye could see, in trucks, in military vehicles, and on foot.

During the afternoon the skies became cloudy and it began to drizzle. Also, the war returned directly to us. First, an artillery duel sent shells whistling over our heads in both directions, and we all hit the dirt, waiting for the explosions. But nothing happened. Gradually we overcame our instinct to duck each time we heard a shell and no longer paid attention to the artillery fire.

Suddenly an ominous roar split the air. We had never heard anything like it before. Then came another roar, and still another. It sounded inhuman, as if hundreds of cattle were roaring in a chorus while being slaughtered. Later, we learned that these roars had come from heavy Soviet rockets called "katyushas."

The drizzle turned into rain. It was getting dark. The front line was inching closer to our ravine. From time to time arcs of fire, accompanied by violent explosions, crisscrossed the black skies. Both armies were firing tracer missiles. We only hoped and prayed that none of those bombs would land in our ravine. Added to this inferno was the clatter of all kinds of vehicles — cars, trucks and tanks — moving westward. It was now pitch dark. At last, the artillery fire subsided. At about 11 o'clock we decided that we were now directly on the front line and would have to go elsewhere, for even if the Germans did not get us now, the Russians almost certainly would.

Since I was the man most familiar with this terrain, I took command. I ordered my men to move out of the ravine and head for the village of Trzydnik, which, according to my calculations, should already have been captured by the Russians.

I instructed the men not to turn back if they were attacked, but to keep pushing forward as rapidly as possible. I also ordered them not to return fire unless they were sure they had come face to face with German troops.

We climbed out of the ravine. By now it was so dark that I could see only the shadows of the people nearest to me, no more than ten feet away. For about ten minutes we moved in silence, our weapons at the ready. Suddenly we heard a command in German, "Halt! Who goes there?" We threw ourselves to the ground and lay there, motionless. Then the same German voice spoke again. "Whoever you are, proceed to the right! Let's stay out of each other's way. The war will soon be over. We all want to live." Then, silence again. I still did not dare to move. But finally I got up and looked around. There was no one in sight. My men were moving forward again. I tried to orient myself. I knew there should have been a dirt road to my left but the field had been so thoroughly plowed up by the heavy tanks and military trucks that the ground had become one big mass of marsh. I kept moving.

Then I froze in my tracks. Someone was moaning. There was a man lying on the ground. It turned out to be one of my men. He was known by the underground name of "The Nail." He had been wounded in both legs. I examined his wounds, and when I found that he had no broken bones, I picked him up and told him to lean on me and try to walk. He tried, but he could not use his legs. So I simply slung him over my shoulders and moved on.

I do not know how long I was carrying "The Nail," but the load on my shoulders seemed to become heavier all the time. I came to some bushes and sat down to rest, gently easing "The Nail" to the ground at my side.

Then came a loud command, this time in Russian,

145

"Halt! Who goes there?" I was thunderstruck. I had not expected to meet the Russians so soon. I pushed "The Nail" back into the bushes and motioned to him to be quiet. Then I turned in the direction of the Russian voice. "I am a Polish partisan," I said in Russian.

"No tricks! Just come over here!" the same Russian voice replied.

I attempted to bargain with my opponent. "Let's meet halfway."

"No!" was the answer. "Better do as I tell you. I won't wait for you all night."

I still hesitated. I knew that the Germans had Russian men with them, "Vlassov boys," who, earlier in the war, under the command of the Russian general Vlassov, had betrayed their country and gone over to the German side.

Finally, we did agree to meet halfway. I emerged from the bushes and walked toward the figure standing in front of me. All at once, I found myself surrounded by three or four other Russians, and I was told to place my hands on my head. For the second time in five years, I had become a prisoner of war. The first time, back in 1939, the Germans had caught me. Now it was the Russians.

CHAPTER NINE

Liberation

My captors took me to an abandoned farm house, disarmed me (or so they thought) and asked me some questions. These Russians turned out not to be bad sorts. They treated me to bread, bacon and liberal helpings of vodka. I was as hungry as a wolf and ate like one. They saw that I was tired and allowed me to sit down on the floor to rest. I tried to keep from falling asleep because I was still not sure whether I was indeed safe, but the moment I sat down on the floor, I was asleep like a baby.

I was awakened by a pair of strong hands shaking me by the shoulder. A Russian lieutenant was standing in front of me. "You're Znachor," he said. "We were told by our commanders to look for you, and for 'Grab' and 'Jim.' Now we've found all of you."

"How did you know I am 'Znachor'?" I wanted to know. The Russians explained that they had found "The Nail" asleep in the bushes where I had left him and that he had told them who I was. They returned my weapons to me. At that point I showed the Soviet officer a small gun which I had kept hidden all the time in a double pocket of my pants.

A few hours later I was back with my comrades. We counted our final casualties..."Polka," Alex Syzmanski...The rest had survived.

After the Russians had released me and I had rejoined my comrades, I returned to Rzeczyca and to the Czerkaski and Kaczkowski families, with whom I had been closest while I stayed in that village. After a good meal I enjoyed a good night's sleep — without my boots on, the first time in almost two years. I was taken to Krasnik, where I stayed with Mr. and Mrs. Czerwinski, the owners of the local pharmacy . I saw to it that all my patients were taken care of and that those who required hospitalization were admitted to a community hospital.

In September, 1944, I arrived in Lublin, the provisional capital of the Polish republic-to-be, for a reunion with my partisan friends and General "Rola" Zymierski, who had taken over as chief of staff of the Polish army, and who now attached me to the high command as an "officer for special assignments."

From the very outset, there had been animosity between the Polish army that had been recruited from refugees in the Soviet Union and the partisans who had organized in Poland. Since I was liked and respected by the underground fighters, it was felt that I could help smooth out relationships between the two organizations that would now have to unite in helping rebuild Poland.

Because of my proficiency in the Russian language I was named liaison officer between the former partisans and the Russian commandant in Lublin, General Senchilo. Several weeks later, I was named chief of the personnel department of the Polish army medical corps. I held this post until the end of the war in Europe in May, 1945.

At my request I was relieved of my administrative duties and transferred to strictly medical functions, with the rank of lieutenant-colonel. I became assistant director of the huge surgical unit of the first Regional Army Hospital in Warsaw. I remained in this capacity until my departure for the United States.

For my underground work and my subsequent activities I was awarded several high decorations, including the Grunwald Cross (the highest decoration in the new Polish republic), the Cross of the Brave, the Cross of Poland Reborn *(Polonia Restituta)*, and numerous other medals. But the decoration I treasure most is the Cross of the Partisans.

Of my family, only two brothers had survived. One of them, who had settled in Palestine thirty years earlier, got in touch with me in October 1944. He wrote to me that he and his family were alive and well. My oldest brother, Sioma Temchin, had been a well-known leader in the youth organization of the "Bund" before the war in Warsaw. At the beginning of the war, Sioma had fled into the Russian sector, where he had been incarcerated in a labor camp in Siberia because of his prewar Socialist activities. Now, after five years at hard labor, he had been released and returned to Warsaw. Alas, two other brothers, our father and my wife Mania, had been killed in Pinsk in 1941, when the Germans occupied the city and massacred the Jews.

In Lublin, soon after the liberation, I met Dr. Emil Sommerstein, who was to become my father-in-law. Before the war, Dr. Sommerstein had been a leader of Polish Jewry and a member of the Polish *Sejm* (Parliament). He was an inmate of several Soviet prisons until 1943, when he was released. When the new Polish provisional government was formed in Lublin, he joined it as head of the Department of War Indemnities. In addition, he organized the Central Jewish Committee, which was instrumental in sustaining whatever remained of the Jews and of Jewish life in Poland after the war.

Through him I met his charming daughter Mira, whom I married in June, 1945. Our first child, our son Jack, was born in May, 1946. At that time Dr. Sommerstein was on a mission to the United States as the head of the Central Jewish Committee's delegation to secure assistance for the surviving victims of the Holocaust.

On September 1, 1946, the day he was supposed to board the boat for his return trip to Poland, Dr. Sommerstein suffered a paralytic stroke.

My wife, my infant son and I were given visas to the U.S.A. by Arthur Bliss Lane, who was then the U.S. ambassador to Poland, so that we could hurry to my father-in-law's side. Dr. Sommerstein never recovered from his illness, and we never returned to Poland.

Our daughter, Shelley, was born in New York in July, 1949. That same year I started to practice medicine in Brooklyn, New York. Four years later, in 1953, we moved to a small town in upstate New York that bears the impressive name of Florida. I practiced there for almost a quarter of a century. For the last 15 years of active practice, I was the Medical Director of Orange Co. Home & Infirmary, an institution I helped to plan and build. As such I headed one of the most modern facilities in the state of N.Y. It houses 350 bedridden patients, ca. 150 ambulatory patients, and a staff of ca. 300, including 4 full-time physicians. Unfortunately, age and the hardships of my years in the woods as a partisan have taken their toll. In 1967 I suffered a heart attack and in 1975 underwent heart surgery. In 1977 I retired. Our son Jack is working in motion pictures; Shelley is a teacher in Massachusetts. Mira and I are happy to be alive and to have raised our two children to maturity in peace and freedom and are content to see them make their contribution to the world in which, for better or worse, we all must live together.

CHAPTER TEN

People
I Have Known

SERGEANT SOLDAU

On January 1, 1940, I was taken to Stalag IA. On arrival I was examined by two physicians who were both prisoners of war. They were Dr. Bronislaw Wislicki from Lodz and Dr. Majem from Lwow. I was given a clean bill of health. They did not know what the Germans would do with me, but they advised me, if possible, rather to be processed further by a German than by a certain blond Polish sergeant who was very brutal and enjoyed beating up new prisoners.

As luck would have it, the German sergeant — his name was Soldau — was free when I arrived at the reception desk. He was loud like all other Germans, who never seemed to talk in a normal tone but could only yell. I told him my name. He found my papers, read them carefully, then slapped my face and shouted, "So you're a doctor, are you? You're just another criminal and you'll be treated like one!" He kept hitting and kicking me, but much to my surprise, he seemed to be putting on an act. He did not really hurt me. While he made a big show of beating me, he maneuvered me into a far corner of the room and in a low voice, between punches, told me the charges that had been made against me, so I should know what to say if I was put through another interrogation. His final punch was genuine. I started to bleed from my nose. The sergeant took me to the office supervisor, a German corporal named Apfel. "I think this Jew will behave himself

155

now," he said to the corporal. "I'll assign him to the infirmary."

"No, he's going to Guerken, the penal compound," Apfel decided. That was how I landed in the "penal compound." I did not see Sergeant Soldau again in Guerken. I heard stories of his "brutal" behavior, but after a short time I had forgotten him altogether.

Early in 1942, after my return to Grabowiec from Warsaw, I was at the headquarters of the *Judenrat* in the town of Hrubieszow near Grabowiec, talking to the *Judenrat's* secretary, Mr. Julius Brandt, when a German in civilian clothes entered the office. He shook hands with Mr. Brandt. The German pretended not to pay any attention to me, but from time to time he gave me sidelong looks as if trying to remember where he had seen me before. His face seemed familiar to me also. Mr. Brandt noticed the tension between us. He closed the door of the office. "Do you know each other?" he asked in Polish.

The German turned to me. "Did you have a brother in Stalag IA, a doctor?"

It was Sergeant Soldau!

"No," I replied. "I did not have a brother there. I was the prisoner whom you beat up one day." We shook hands heartily.

It turned out that Soldau had been a master sergeant in the Polish army, who had been taken prisoner and interned in Stalag IA. He pretended to be a *Volksdeutscher*. He helped many of his fellow POW's; for instance, he would pretend to beat up other prisoners so that they would not be beaten by the Germans, but he never hurt anyone, and so he saved me, too, from really being harmed by the Germans. Actually, Soldau was not a *Volksdeutscher* but a Jew.

After his release from the prison camp, he continued the masquerade. His appearance and his German speech were that of a super-Aryan German. He had come to Hrubieszow and been appointed administrator of one of the largest estates in the region that had been confiscated from its Polish owners. He employed many Jews on the estate and treated them well. Mr. Brandt would send him Jews who for some reason had incurred the special disfavor of the German authorities. Soldau (this was his real name) would protect them. After the war I tried to find Soldau, but I never heard anything about him again.

DR. DLUGI

Dr. Henryk Dlugi had been a well-known gynecologist and obstetrician in Vilna before the war. He had served as chief assistant to the noted Professor Jakowicki. When he was taken prisoner, he was assigned to Stalag IA as head of the infirmary in Guerken.

There were many doctors in Guerken, among them a Dr. Wilk, who had been a pediatric surgeon at the children's hospital on Sliska Street in Warsaw. But Dr. Dlugi was the doctor most liked and respected by his patients, his colleagues and, most important, by the German head of the hospital and infirmary, who was impressed by Dlugi's knowledge, honesty and forthrightness.

I had met Dr. Dlugi several days after my arrival at Stalag IA, told him of my predicament and asked him for help. At first, when he tried to intervene with the German doctor, he could do nothing for me. That was why I had to stay in the "penal compound" as long as I did. I probably would have starved to death if it had not been for Dr. Dlugi, who sent me food packages and, occasionally, when I visited the infirmary, gave me some warm soup he had saved for me.

On March 30, 1940, when I was exhausted, sick and certain that I would not survive the day, Dlugi sent a messenger ordering me to come to the infirmary at once and bring all my belongings. I obeyed.

At the infirmary there was a German doctor looking for a multilingual physician. I qualified, and Dr. Dlugi took advantage of the situation to ship me out of the camp. The German doctor did not say anything. Dr. Dlugi helped me into the car and gave me his own blanket (mine could walk by itself since it was crawling with lice). I asked him where I was going. His angry answer was, "I don't know, but wherever you go it will be better than here. If you stay you'll be dead in a matter of days. So don't be choosy." The car moved and I left — was it for better or for worse?

About two or three months after my departure. Dr. Dlugi was released and went back to Vilna.

In 1947, when I moved into an apartment on West End Avenue and 101st Street in New York City with my father-in-law, Dr. Emil Sommerstein, my second wife and our young son, Dr. Dlugi and his family were our neighbors. We became good friends and remained so until his untimely death.

DR. MED. MAJOR CLEMENS HANTEL

Dr. Dlugi was right. I should have been happy to be taken out of the "penal compound." There, I would not have lasted much longer. Besides, I had no choice. My new patron apparently did not believe in bureaucratic red tape. We left Guerken, passed the main office and drove on. For about fifteen minutes, neither of us uttered a word. Then, without turning his face from the road, he handed me an apple. "You must be hungry," he said. "Take this. There's also some chocolate in the glove compartment." I was hungry and this was an unexpected good beginning. But, I wondered, what will happen when he finds out I'm a Jew? I did not want to make a point of it, but at the same time I did not want to be accused of hiding my Jewishness. So I decided to come out with the truth then and there. When the major asked my name, I replied, "Moses Temchin. I'm a Jew."

"I didn't ask you about your religion," Hantel replied. "All I wanted to know was your name. As far as I'm concerned, you are a Polish officer, a doctor, and a prisoner of war, and you will be treated as such. In the future, you will answer all questions specifically and not volunteer any other information."

The major's name was Clemens Hantel. A reserve officer, he was stationed in the small town of Guttstadt not far from Allenstein and Koenigsberg and was in charge of medical services for about 6,000 French, and Polish prisoners of war, as well as for some civilians, mostly Poles working on farms, factories and highway construction projects. He spoke only German. He needed help, and I was glad he had found me. During our trip I learned that I would live at the community hospital run by Catholic nuns, and would have an entire wing in the main building for my patients and a smaller unit for communicable diseases in another building.

We arrived in Guttstadt at about five o'clock that afternoon. Hantel introduced me to the nuns, who took me to my quarters.

When I saw my room I thought it was a dream. A rather large room, all white. There was a metal hospital bed, a night table with a bell and a telephone. On the bed lay a pair of pajamas and a bathrobe. The nuns suggested that after they had left I should undress completely, put on the bathrobe and leave my uniform and other belongings on the floor.

Then they showed me the bathroom and left. After a refreshing shower, I put on my pajamas and returned to my room. There I found a clean shirt, a pair of fresh woolen socks, and my own uniform, cleaned and deloused.

Afterwards, I was served dinner. I remember it was pea soup with bacon. I ate two full plates. I was told I could not have a third helping because there were still meat and dessert to come. I ate it all. I was still hungry, but I was ashamed to ask for more. The nuns watched me, smiled, and probably wondered when I had eaten or slept last. After dinner. I went to bed and slept like a baby.

About eight o'clock the next morning Hantel came and showed me around. The hospital was small but well

161

equipped. Dr. Hantel was always available for consultations if needed, but I had complete control over procedures and treatment.

Within a short time Dr. Hantel and I became great friends. He confided to me that he had never given the Hitler salute in his life, that he hated the Fuehrer and all he stood for, and that his wife and two children shared his feelings. He invited me to his house where I met his family.

In May or early June, 1940, the Germans announced that civilians who were suffering from chronic diseases or were otherwise unable to work would be released and sent home. I used the opportunity to give as many diagnoses of chronic disease as possible—ulcers, sprained backs and the like—and so was able to send many prisoners back to their homes in the *Generalgouvernement,* the German-occupied sector of Poland. I was especially eager to see one prisoner, Felix Krawiec, sent home to Warsaw. Krawiec pretended to be a Catholic but was a Jew and I was afraid that sooner or later someone would denounce him to the Germans. Since the inmates had no money but were required to pay for their own transportation, I often paid their fare from my salary. In one instance, when I ran out of money, Dr. Hantel "financed" two repatriates. When I asked him why he should want to do that, he replied. "Let the future Polish government be obligated to me even in some small way. Then they might treat me with some consideration after the war."

In our frequent political discussions, Dr. Hantel told me that, as a German, he prayed for his fatherland but he knew in his heart that Germany would lose the war and pay dearly for what she had done. His only consolation was that Hitler and his cohorts would vanish from the face of the earth.

162

Dr. Hantel was like a father and protector to me. There was one incident that could have cost my life if it had not been for Dr. Hantel. The Polish prisoners of war and civilians in Guttstadt were allowed to attend services at the Catholic church on Sunday. Before going to church, they would visit coworkers and me, their doctor, at the hospital. One Sunday after services, a German soldier, who was drunk, asked the Polish people to sing something in Polish. They obliged and suddenly the small church rang with a hymn that was not part of the Catholic liturgy:

> *Nie damy ziemi . . .*
> *Nie damy dzieci germanic*
> *Tak nam dopomoz Bog . . .*

"We won't give up the land . . .
We won't let you Germanize our children . . .
So help us God . . ."

The services were stopped at once. Several hours later, the German police came to interrogate me. They accused me of having incited the demonstration. At that point Major Hantel, in full uniform, with all his decorations, entered the room. "Dr. Temchin is my responsibility and under my jurisdiction," he said. Without another word, my interrogators vanished and I was left alone.

The following year in Warsaw, I wrote to St. Joseph's Hospital, requesting a letter describing my professional activities there. On February 8, 1941, I received a letter over the signature of Dr. Hantel, testifying to the excellent work I had done at his hospital.

In May, 1945, after the liberation of East Prussia, I went to Guttstadt to look for Dr. Hantel and for the nuns. The town was almost completely in ruins and no one could tell me what had become of my protectors.

163

In New York, in 1951, I met a friend and classmate of mine, Dr. Michael Bryce, who had been the last doctor after me in Guttstadt, had survived the war and opened a practice in Manhattan. Bryce had only the highest praise for Dr. Hantel. Unfortunately, he told me, Hantel was no longer alive. In 1943, he had developed severe abdominal pains. No definite diagnosis could be made, and an operation was performed. It turned out that he had a perforated duodenal ulcer. He died several days later. His family left Guttstadt and settled somewhere in West Germany. If ever there was a righteous man, his name was *Reservemajor der Wehrmacht* Dr.med. Clemens Hantel.

ELE

I was asleep on my pallet at the labor camp in Biala Podlaska when I was rudely shaken awake by a pair of strong hands. When I opened my eyes I saw a muscular man, about six feet tall, half naked and smelling of a mixture of sweat and vodka.

"I am Ele," he told me, "and we need a doctor." I had heard that name before. Everyone knew Ele Baumsecer. Before the war, he had been a notorious criminal in Warsaw's Jewish underworld. Now, at Podlaska, he was catering to the SS and other guards. His "work" at this labor camp was to procure good food, alcohol and girls for the German overlords. In return, he was given certain privileges and sometimes was able to help his fellow prisoners.

This time someone was sick with severe abdominal pains and vomiting. I examined the man and diagnosed acute appendicitis. Ele had the man transported to a Jewish hospital that still existed nearby and the man was operated on. From then on, Ele became my best friend. Who was Ele? Before the war, the Jews of Warsaw had their famous synagogues, a fine Judaic institute, elegant restaurants, their own theatres and — Krochmalna Street. On one end of this thoroughfare was the headquarters of the *Kehilla*, the official Jewish community, but starting from the corner of Ciepla, toward Zelazna and onward, Krochmalna turned into the capital of the Jewish underworld, swarming with Jewish prostitutes, pimps, thieves and pickpockets. The Jewish underworld was not known for murders, but safecracking, pickpocketing and prostitution flourished there. (There was, however, one typically "Jewish " attitude that was not found among Gentile criminals. In certain cases one could negotiate for the return of stolen goods if one could convince the thieves that their victim was poor and that the theft had therefore been an act of real injustice.) My friend Ele was the king of Krochmalna Street, even as his father and grandfather had been before him.

After the liquidation of the Biala Podlaska camp Ele was to return to Warsaw, where he started "working the wall," soon taking over most of the smuggling operations between the ghetto and the "Aryan sector." His headquarters were on Elektoralna and Ptasia Streets. In the summer of 1942, when I myself had come to Warsaw, I heard that Ele had been inquiring about me. I went to see him. He was elegantly dressed in a leather jacket and new officer's boots. He greeted me with a big hug and kiss. "This is the doctor I've been telling you about," he kept on announcing to his collaborators. He invited me for dinner. Though my family in Pinsk had not been rich, we had always eaten very well, but what I was served at Ele's headquarters surpassed my imagination. There were sardines, herring with onions, tomatoes, gefilte fish, roast goose with stuffing and vegetables, all washed down with prewar vodka. For dessert there were sweets and, after that, an assortment of blondes and brunettes. At the risk of offending my host, I refused the latter delicacies. But he understood. I was not to see him or hear from him again until the day the "Little Ghetto" of Warsaw was liquidated.

Ele's family was not particularly illustrious. His mother, his sisters and his fiancee had all been prostitutes. But they were his flesh and blood, and he refused to leave them, not even to save himself.

* * *

After the war I heard two versions of Ele's fate. One was that he went to Treblinka and perished. The other version, which I tend to accept more readily, was that he escaped from the *Umschlagplatz* and became an avenger of Jewish lives, killing mostly gendarmes in and out of the ghetto, and that, in April, 1943, he participated in the Warsaw ghetto uprising.

There was, and I imagine still is, considerable difference of opinion regarding individuals like Ele and other small-time smugglers. True, they enriched themselves from the miseries of others. They were parasites and criminals. On the other hand, these people were the only suppliers of whatever food there was in the ghetto, and so they enabled many other Jews to survive, risking their own lives in the process.

Was their action justified? Was their behavior moral? I think the argument will go on and on like so many other arguments about problems left in the wake of the Holocaust. I do not have the answer and am in no position to pass judgment.

DR. HIRSCH—WISNIEWSKI

The train transporting Jews from Grojec stopped and unloaded at the Gdansk railroad station in Warsaw. From there, we all marched to the delousing station on Leszno Street, not far from Zelazna. Usually, I was told, this procedure took only a few hours, but since we had arrived late in the afternoon, we were forced to spend all that night at this "delightful" institution.

At about midnight, I developed a severe toothache. I asked the attendants at the delousing station for something to kill the pain. They referred me to the house doctor. I opened a door marked with a piece of paper on which was scrawled the word *Arzt* (Physician). Inside, there was a man of about seventy, bald, undernourished, looking more like a Polish landowner than a doctor. I told him my problem, but all he could do for me was to give me the last aspirin tablet he possessed. The delousing station had to have a doctor, and this old man had been chosen for the job. But apparently the rules had said nothing about medication, and so the doctor had no medicines to give.

We introduced ourselves to each other. His name was Dr. Hirsch-Wisniewski. He told me that he was a dermatologist and that, for many years before the war, he had been the head of a *kasa chorych* (labor union clinic) on Wolska Street.

Two years later, in 1943, when I came to Rzeczyca, near Lublin, my partisan comrade "Jim" (his real name was

168

Waclaw Czyzewski) told me that there was a doctor in the village, an old man who had come from Warsaw. He was living with a peasant family. Jim thought that this doctor was Jewish. Until the previous winter, he had been busy treating partisans in the woods, but he had been doing nothing lately because he was obviously failing.

I went to see the old doctor. It was my friend from the delousing station. It turned out that when his Gentile maid, who had been with him for many years, lost her father, she gave him her father's birth certificate. The dead man's name had been Wisniewski, and it was with this document and Aryan name that Dr. Hirsch had left the Warsaw ghetto and made his way into the Lublin woods. I visited him whenever possible, which meant: very rarely.

When the fighting in the Lublin region came to an end and I became chief of personnel of the Polish army medical corps, Dr. Hirsch-Wisniewski appeared in my office and presented me with his documents from World War I, stating that he had served as an inspector of field hospitals in the Tsarist army, with the rank of colonel. Now he demanded official recognition of his former rank and function. I received permission from the commander, General "Rola" Zymierski, to give the old man official status. The doctor was elated. He did more traveling than actual inspecting, particularly since he liked flying. His entire outlook and appearance changed. He seemed twenty years younger and with his thick mustache, and his new uniform with the insignia of a colonel, he looked every inch the officer and gentleman he was supposed to be. As I said before, he enjoyed flying. Late in 1944, he died in an airplane crash.

GENERAL SENCHILO

After the liberation of the Lublin region, I joined the regular Polish army and was attached to the high command as an officer for special assignments. I was well known and liked by the partisans and whenever there was trouble involving a partisan and the army, they would turn to me. One night I was awakened by one of our boys, "Pietruszka," a native of Lublin, who had settled down with his family in a small house on the outskirts of the city. His wife was pregnant.

It seemed that a group of drunken Russian soldiers had tried to break into his house. They needed a woman. "Pietruszka" pleaded with them, telling them who he was and that the woman they wanted was his own wife, but it did not help. They broke in the door. Pietruszka had no choice. He greeted them with a burst of fire from his machine gun, grabbed his family and ran.

I arranged for "Pietruszka" and his wife to be driven in a military truck with a partisan driver to Lubartow, a town about thirty kilometers away. Then I went back to sleep.

At about eight o'clock in the morning, I was awakened again. General Senchilo, the Russian commandant of the city, wanted to see me. I dressed and went to see the general.

General Senchilo was a jovial-looking, rather rotund, medium-sized man. He extended his hand to me in a very cordial fashion and, with a broad smile, said, "So you are

170

'Znachor'? Ha? I've wanted to meet you for a long time, but you know how busy we are. Have you had breakfast?"

"No, I did not," I replied.

"Good," he said. "We'll have breakfast together, then." On his order an aide brought in sardines, cold cuts, eggs, coffee and, of course, vodka. The food was excellent and we both enjoyed the meal. He asked me about myself, my family, and partisan life. In between courses we drank to each other's health and wondered what the "brave new world" we were now engaged in building would look like. The general had not yet said a word about his reason for wanting to see me. But I knew it would come up eventually. After about an hour or so, I looked at my watch and said, "General, I thank you for your hospitality. It was a pleasure, but it is late, and I have a lot of work to do." The general got up, looked at his own watch, and agreed with me that it was late. He said that our time together had been most pleasantly spent, but then all good things must come to an end. We shook hands very firmly and I opened the door of the general's office to leave.

Just as I was about to close the door behind me from the outside, the general spoke. "By the way, did you hear what happened to our Russian soldiers last night? Did you know that some of our men were killed and wounded by one of your ex-partisans?"

"I know," I calmly replied.

"Well, so you'll turn the man over to us and we'll deal with him in our own way," said the general.

"No, I won't do that," I answered.

"And why not?" the general wanted to know.

I looked him directly in the eye and said, "General, do you have a wife, or a daughter?"

"Of course," he said and began to rummage in his pockets, probably for a family photograph.

171

"What would you do if drunken hooligans would want to rape them?" I asked.

"Why, I would kill them, of course," said General Senchilo.

"Well," I retorted, "that's exactly what Pietruszka did."

Senchilo was flabbergasted. He looked at me intently, thought for a while and then said, "*Nu—pravda*" ("Well, I suppose you're right"). There was a twinkle in his eye as he slowly closed the door behind me.

He never mentioned the incident to me again.

REDHEADS, BLONDS

At the outset of the war, in 1939, when it became clear that the battle for Poland was lost, all able-bodied Poles were advised to go east, toward the Russian border. They did not have to go far, since the Russians entered Poland from the east.

Almost all the men, and even entire families, were seized by the Russians and sent farther east, mostly to Siberia and other parts of Asiatic Russia. As a result, many families became separated and lost contact with each other.

* * *

My office, the personnel office of the Polish army medical corps, was in possession of a list of Polish doctors and related professionals who had fled to Russia during the war; this list included the names of Polish doctors in the Russian army. The list helped me to locate some of these men, both Jewish and Gentile, and reunite them with their families. My office saw tears and misery in plenty when I could not locate a husband or father on my list, but there were also tears of happiness when I succeeded in bringing families together.

* * *

In America a redhead is usually considered a beautiful person, someone to admire. But in Poland, red was not a popular shade, at least not as far as hair was concerned. We called redheads *gayl* ("yellow") in Yiddish and *rudy* in Polish. I am citing this observation because on this particular occasion my perception of the color of a man's hair almost prevented a happy family reunion.

One morning when I arrived at my office — it was about 8:30 — my secretary informed me that there was an old woman waiting for me. "Is she good-looking?" I asked jokingly.

"No," the girl replied. "She's old, very timid and, in general, she looks a mess. Also, she is a redhead."

I entered the room. My secretary was right. There was a red-haired women, very thin, pale and old-looking. I noted that she seemed dehydrated and very frightened. She told me her name. Her husband, Dr. M., a doctor from a town in Galicia, and his unmarried brother, a dentist, had fled east in the fall of 1939 and she had not heard from either of them since.

Dr. M. and the dentist M., both of Galicia? I happened to know that both of them were alive. They had, in fact, arrived in Lublin from Siberia only the day before. They had come to my office in search of their families, but had been told that all their relatives had perished.

Now I had wonderful news for both of them, and for the red-haired woman who was sitting in my office. But I did not want to tell it to this woman without first preparing her. I had known of cases where people collapsed in my office from sheer happiness on learning that loved ones who they thought had died in the war were still alive.

So I began to speak slowly and very casually. "Dr. M., and his brother, the dentist M.? Yes, I knew them before the war. In fact, I heard their names mentioned not too long ago." I acted as if I were trying to remember where I had heard the name.

Mrs. M. was quite excited. "You say you know them?" she cried. "You've heard of them? Oh God—please tell me! What happened to them?" Suddenly, she seemed younger and more elegant, even in the shabby dress she was wearing.

I had one more question to ask her. "Is your husband a redhead?"

She blushed and looked down at her hands. "No! My husband a redhead? Never! He's blond." She spoke as if she would consider it a downright disgrace if he, like herself, were a redhead.

I almost burst out laughing, but restrained myself. "What a pity," I said. "If he were a redhead, then I could tell you that I saw him only yesterday and that I know where he is now. The man I saw is a redhead—really red, an ugly red."

The woman leaped from her chair. "Where is he?" she almost screamed. "Where is my husband?"

I made her sit down and tried to calm her. Now she was crying, and so was my secretary while she wrote down the address of Mrs. M.'s husband. A few days later I saw all the three of them together, the two brothers and the doctor's wife. Despite their red hair, they seemed to me good-looking and very, very happy.

* * *

Warsaw was liberated on January 17, 1945. The headquarters of the Polish army moved to the little town of Wlochy. My office was transferred to Tworki and had taken over a very modern building that had previously

175

housed a mental institution. There were still many Polish doctors not accounted for, and I still was in a position to find some of them.

The second in command at my office was a major by the name of Dzigora. One afternoon there was not much business going on. My secretary came in to say that a client was waiting for me. "What a beauty!" she exclaimed. "She's lovely, elegant and faultlessly made-up, a real prima donna."

When the lady came in, Major Dzigora and I agreed that my secretary had not been exaggerating. The lady introduced herself and told me her story. Several months before the war, she had married a dentist. In September, 1939, her bridegroom had fled to the east and she had never heard from him again. Somehow, she had managed to survive the war. She was, frankly, less concerned about her husband than about her marital status. She wanted to know exactly where she stood. If her husband was dead, she wanted to find out the truth because she was still young and attractive and did not want to pass up any chances of rebuilding her life.

She informed me that she was living alone, not far from my office, in a furnished room with a separate entrance, a piano and a phonograph. And she always had something good to drink for her visitors. If I was not too busy that night or the next, I would be most welcome at her place.

Since I was then already engaged to the girl who was to become my second wife, this was out of the question. "But really, Colonel . . . " our visitor murmured, "Why on earth not?"

"Write down her address anyway," Major Dzigora whispered to me in Russian. "If you don't want to go yourself, I will gladly accept her invitation." He wrote down the address on a slip of paper and put it into his uniform pocket. Two hours after the woman had left, her husband turned up in my office. He had come back to Warsaw and, believing that his wife had died, enlisted in the Polish army. I told him that his wife was still alive. Major Dzigora removed the slip of paper with the address from his pocket and slowly tore it to bits.

I do not know what happened that evening in the furnished room with the separate entrance, the piano and the phonograph, but a few months later I learned that the couple had decided to get a divorce.

BULGANIN

One day, a Russian major visited me in my office. He told me that he was attached to the political department of the Polish army, and that I had caused him a lot of trouble. The day before, a blonde, very attractive young female physician had been assigned by my office to an infantry unit stationed some distance away from Lublin. The problem, according to the major, was that she should have been kept in Lublin. It was imperative that she be returned to Lublin. When I asked the major what was so important about her, he bluntly indicated that this was none of my business. It was, he said, a decision of the political department. I did not like his answer. I suspected the reason for his interest in this girl, but I did not want to put him on the spot.

However, I refused to have the girl transferred back to Lublin. I told the major that while it was none of my business why he wanted this transfer so badly, I had to have some official statement on paper to justify my removing her from an assignment where she was badly needed and bringing her back to Lublin, where, at the moment, there was nothing for her to do. The major became angry and left the room in a huff, uttering the famous Russian "last word," *Uvidim* ("We'll see about that").

The next day I received a telephone call from a colonel in the political department of the Polish army, instructing me to arrange for the young woman's transfer immediately. Again, I said I could do nothing unless I received an official written directive from the political department. This conversation, too, ended with the colonel saying, *"Uvidim."*

About a week later my immediate superior, General Moguchi, the chief of the medical corps of the Polish army, called me to the telephone. It seemed that General (as he was then) Bulganin was on the line and wanted to talk to me. Bulganin was a liaison officer between the Polish and Soviet armies.

"What's going on in that personnel department of yours?" the voice on the telephone demanded. I did not like his tone.

"Who is this speaking?" I asked.

"This is General Bulganin."

I decided to play dumb. "Are you in the Polish army or in the Red Army?" I inquired.

"I am General Bulganin of the Red Army," came the reply.

"In that case," I said, "I must tell you that I cannot transmit any information to an officer in a foreign army without direct orders from my own chief of staff. I am sorry, but I shall supply whatever information you need only if I receive written orders from General Zymierski."

"I see," said Bulganin and hung up.

That afternoon the Russian major showed up in my office again. He apologized for his behavior. He explained that the young "physician-lieutenant" was his girlfriend and that he wanted her close by. However, he now realized that he had gone about it the wrong way and appealed to my sense of camaraderie.

I relented, found a new assignment for her, and a few days later, the young woman doctor was back in Lublin.

About a week later "Rola" Zymierski called me and invited me, as one of his aides, to accompany him to a party at the Soviet military mission. I polished my boots and, at seven o'clock that evening I joined him to go to the party.

General Bulganin was one of the guests, and I was introduced to him as "Major Temchin." But after a few vodkas, General Zymierski asked Bulganin whether he knew who I was. Of course he knew, Bulganin replied. He had just met Major Temchin. "No, you're wrong," said Zymierski. "This is Znachor."

"Znachor, you old son of a gun!" Bulganin shouted and slapped me on the shoulder. "Tell me, how is the major, and how is the 'physician lieutenant'?"

"They're together now," I replied.

"That's good," said General Bulganin.

GOMULKA

One day in February or March, 1945, I received a telephone call from General "Rola" Zymierski, the chief of staff of the Polish army. He informed me that Wladyslaw Gomulka, the Communist party chief, was suffering from paralysis of the face. Zymierski wanted me to arrange a consultation with the best medical men in the army.

I immediately summoned a neurologist, a surgeon, an internist and an otolaryngologist, all known specialists in their respective fields, and arranged for us to meet at Gomulka's home. When we arrived there we were met by a group of civilian doctors, who had been assembled there by Gomulka's personal physician, Dr. G. I could only stare in amazement at this crowd of doctors, in and out of uniform. There were definitely too many doctors and I was afraid that whatever was wrong with Gomulka would only get worse after all of us had finished with him.

The apartment was small and shabby. Mrs. Gomulka was embarrassed because she could not find room and chairs for all of us. After mutual introductions and an exchange of ceremonial niceties, the examination of the patient began.

Mr. Gomulka was in bed. He was feeling fine, except that the left side of his face was deformed. He had difficulty closing his mouth and was unable to close his eye on the affected side.

Each doctor put him through a thorough examination. I do not know in what order the civilian doctors approached him, but in the case of the military doctors, the answer was simple — the highest-ranking officers were the first to be admitted to the patient's bedside. Since all the other army doctors were generals, while I was only a major, they all entered the bedroom before me. I went in last. I did not want to examine him; I thought he had had enough for one session.

After partaking of sandwiches and coffee prepared by Mrs. Gomulka, we all sat down and discussed the findings. Our diagnosis was clear: paralysis of the facial nerve. But what had caused the trouble? Some suggested that Gomulka might have a tumor. Others opted for syphilis, tuberculosis and a variety of other conditions.

I was the last to speak up. "Gentlemen," I said, "according to my own limited experience, I would say that what we have here is a fairly common condition, rather harmless, probably rheumatic in origin. Just because our patient happens to be Wladyslaw Gomulka, does he have to have all the dreadful diseases we have just enumerated? If this patient were a private in a battalion, he would be given three days' sick leave, six to eight aspirins daily and then sent back to his duties. In my opinion, this is exactly what should be done also in this case."

At this moment the door of Gomulka's bedroom opened and there stood our patient, dressed only in his nightshirt. He stretched out his arm and pointed to the apartment door. "Out! Out! All of you!" he shouted. We did not have to be told that twice and quickly left the Gomulka residence.

Three days later, Gomulka was back at his desk.

CHIEF RABBI OF THE POLISH ARMY

At the end of the war, the part of Poland occupied by the Soviets was officially annexed by U.S.S.R. and was sealed off from what formerly had been the German-occupied sector. No one could cross the border in either direction. Many Jews, Poles and Ukrainians were thus trapped in Russia without any hope of being able to return to Poland in the near future.

Among these unfortunates were Rabbi David Kahana and his family. The Kahanas had been good friends of my future father-in-law, Dr. Emil Sommerstein. When Dr. Sommerstein learned that the rabbi had survived the Holocaust, he was anxious to bring him back to Poland.

(At this point I would like to pay tribute to the Metropolitan Andrew Szeptycki, whose heroism, compassion and humanitarianism were largely responsible for the survival of Rabbi Kahana and his family. Throughout the period of German occupation, Szeptycki kept Rabbi Kahana and his wife safe in a monasterty. The rabbi, dressed as a monk, worked as a librarian in the monastery, while his wife was employed in the kitchen. In addition, the Metropolitan had placed into that same monastery some seventy Jewish orphans, who were given shelter by the monks under his personal patronage.)

As a member of the Polish provisional government, Dr. Sommerstein attempted to intercede with the Polish and Russian authorities on Rabbi Kahana's behalf, but to no avail. The Russians refused to let the rabbi return to Poland. So, eventually, Dr. Sommerstein turned to me for help.

Before long, I found a way to bring Rabbi Kahana home. The new Polish army had a religious department with Catholic and Orthodox chaplains, but nothing had been said about naming a Jewish chaplain. I decided to discuss this matter with General Zymierski.

The general expressed surprise; he had not been aware that there was no Jewish chaplain in the Polish army. Did I have a candidate in mind for the position? He would have to be a man of stature, well spoken and cultured. I said I had exactly the man for the job, Rabbi Kahana. However, there was one slight difficulty: he was still in Russia. "That should be no problem," General Zymierski replied, and immediately requested Rabbi Kahana's repatriation to Poland on the grounds that he was liable to service in the Polish army.

A military plane was dispatched to pick up Rabbi Kahana in Lwow. The following day he was given the rank of major and officially appointed chief Jewish chaplain in the Polish army.

It was Rabbi Kahana who, in June, 1945, solemnized my marriage to Mira Sommerstein.

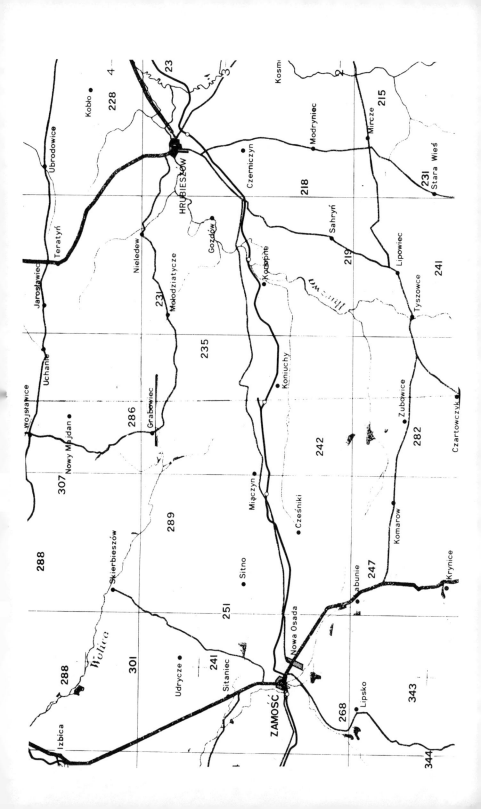